MathFlare

Name: _______________________

Class: ___________

Teacher: _______________________

Introduction

As parents and educators, we recognize the pivotal role mathematics plays in shaping a child's academic journey and future success. Yet, the path to mathematical proficiency can often seem daunting, fraught with challenges and complexities. That's where the transformative power of MathFlare Workbooks shine through, illuminating the way forward with clarity, precision, and purpose.

Introducing MathFlare Workbooks – a beacon of guidance, a testament to excellence, and a catalyst for achievement. Crafted with meticulous care and expertise, MathFlare Workbooks stand as paragons of educational excellence, designed to nurture young minds, ignite a passion for learning, and develop a deep-rooted understanding of mathematical concepts.

Picture this: your child eagerly delves into the pages of Mathflare Workbook, greeted by a step-by-step guide illuminated with vivid examples that demystify complex mathematical concepts. With each turn of the page, they embark on a journey of discovery, encountering thoughtfully curated practice questions that reinforce learning and hone problem-solving skills. And when they unveil the answers to those very questions, a sense of accomplishment blossoms within them – a tangible reward for their hard work and dedication.

But MathFlare Workbooks are more than just tools for learning; they are pathways to comprehension, fostering a deep-seated understanding of mathematical concepts through a sequential, logical flow. From fundamental principles to advanced problem-solving strategies, every chapter builds upon the last, ensuring a robust foundation upon which future knowledge can be constructed.

As parents, we yearn for nothing more than to see our children thrive, to witness the spark of inspiration ignited within them as they conquer academic challenges with confidence and poise. MathFlare Workbooks serve as partners in this noble endeavor, offering not just practice questions, but the keys to unlocking a world of opportunity.

And for teachers, MathFlare Workbooks stand as invaluable allies in the quest to cultivate mathematical proficiency in the classroom. With answers readily available, instructors can focus on guiding and nurturing their students, confident in the knowledge that MathFlare Workbooks provide a solid framework upon which to build.

In the pages of MathFlare Workbooks, we find not just the promise of academic excellence, but the seeds of a brighter tomorrow. So let us embrace the power of mathematics, let us champion the journey of learning, and let us pave the way for a generation of young minds poised to shape the world. With MathFlare Workbooks as our guide, the possibilities are infinite, and the future, bright.

Table of Contents

MathFlare
MATH WORKBOOK
Grade 2
Step by Step Guide and Essential Practice with Answers
Addition Subtraction
Multiplication
Place Value and Expanded Notations
Geometry
MathFlare Publishing

MathFlare
MATH WORKBOOK
Grade 2-3
Step by Step Guide and Essential Practice with Answers
Addition Subtraction
Multiplication and Division
Place Value and Expanded Notations
Geometry
MathFlare Publishing

MathFlare
MATH WORKBOOK
Grade 3
Step by Step Guide and Essential Practice with Answers
Multiplication and Division
Decimals
Place Value and Expanded Notations
Fractions and Geometry
MathFlare Publishing

MathFlare
MATH WORKBOOK
Grade 1
Step by Step Guide and Essential Practice with Answers
Counting and Numbers
Addition and Subtraction
Place Value and Expanded Notations
Understanding Time
MathFlare Publishing

MathFlare
MATH WORKBOOK
Grade 1-2
Step by Step Guide and Essential Practice with Answers
Counting and Numbers
Addition and Subtraction
Place Value and Expanded Notations
Understanding Time
MathFlare Publishing

MathFlare
MATH WORKBOOK
Grade 3-4
Step by Step Guide and Essential Practice with Answers
Addition Subtraction
Multiplication Division
Place Value and Expanded Notations
Fractions and Geometry
MathFlare Publishing

MathFlare
MATH WORKBOOK
Grade 4
Step by Step Guide and Essential Practice with Answers
Addition Subtraction
Multiplication Division
Place Value and Expanded Notations
Fractions and Geometry
MathFlare Publishing

MathFlare
MATH WORKBOOK
Grade 4-5
Step by Step Guide and Essential Practice with Answers
Multiplication Division
Place Value and Expanded Notations
Fractions and Geometry
Unit Conversion
MathFlare Publishing

MathFlare
MATH WORKBOOK
5
Step by Step Guide and Essential Practice with Answers
Multiplication Division
Place Value and Expanded Notations
Fractions and Geometry
Unit Conversion
MathFlare Publishing

MathFlare
MATH WORKBOOK
5-6
Step by Step Guide and Essential Practice with Answers
Multiplication Division
Place Value and Expanded Notations
Fractions and Geometry
Units and Statistics
MathFlare Publishing

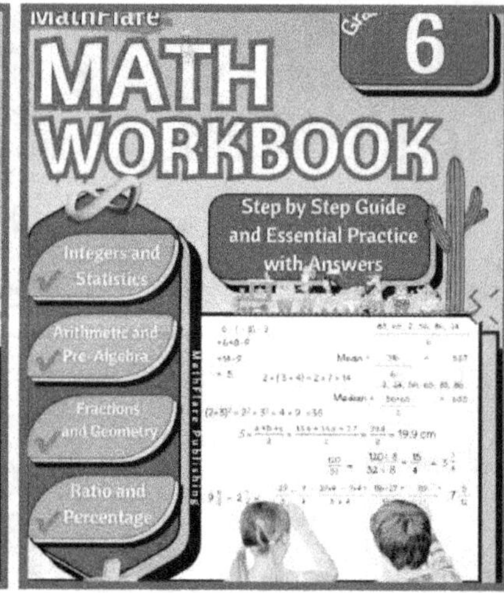
MathFlare
MATH WORKBOOK
6
Step by Step Guide and Essential Practice with Answers
Integers and Statistics
Arithmetic and Pre-Algebra
Fractions and Geometry
Ratio and Percentage
MathFlare Publishing

MathFlare
MATH WORKBOOK
6-7
Step by Step Guide and Essential Practice with Answers
Arithmetic and Pre-Algebra
Ratio, Percent Proportion
Geometry
Statistics
MathFlare Publishing

MathFlare
MATH WORKBOOK
7
Step by Step Guide and Essential Practice with Answers
Pre-Algebra
Ratio, Percent Proportion
Geometry
Statistics
MathFlare Publishing

MathFlare
MATH WORKBOOK
7-8
Step by Step Guide and Essential Practice with Answers
Pre-Algebra
Ratio, Percent Proportion
Geometry and Cartesian Plane
Statistics
MathFlare Publishing

MathFlare
MATH WORKBOOK
8-9
Step by Step Guide and Essential Practice with Answers
Pre-Algebra
Ratio, Proportion and Percentage
Linear Equations
Geometry and Cartesian Plane
MathFlare Publishing

MathFlare
MATH WORKBOOK
8
Step by Step Guide and Essential Practice with Answers
Pre-Algebra
Percentage
Linear Equations
Geometry
MathFlare Publishing

Positive and Negative Integers

Positive and negative integers are whole numbers that can represent quantities greater than zero and less than zero, respectively.

Positive Integers: Positive integers are whole numbers greater than zero. They are denoted by the numbers 1,2,3,4...

Negative Integers: Negative integers are whole numbers less than zero. They are denoted by placing a negative sign ("-") before the numbers, such as $-1, -2, -3, -4,...$

The positive integers are used to represent the number of objects, scores, etc. whereas the negative integers can be used to represent debt, losses, temperatures below freezing points, etc.

Let's solve some problems:

1. $6 - (-8) - 9$

- Start by simplifying within the parentheses:

$$-(-8) \text{ becomes } 8.$$

- Rewrite the expression with the simplified part:

$$6 + 8 - 9.$$

- Now perform addition and subtraction from left to right:

$$6 + 8 = 14, \text{ then } 14 - 9 = 5$$

2. $(-5) - (-3) + 10$

$$(-5) + 3 + 10$$

$$(-5) + 3 = -2, \text{ then } -2 + 10 = 8$$

Order of Operations (PEMDAS)

The order of operations, often remembered by the acronym PEMDAS, stands for:

- **Parentheses**: Perform operations inside parentheses first.
- **Exponents**: Evaluate exponents (powers and roots) next.
- **Multiplication and Division**: Perform multiplication and division from left to right.
- **Addition and Subtraction**: Perform addition and subtraction from left to right.

The order of operations helps to clarify which operations should be performed first in a mathematical expression to ensure consistent and accurate results.

- **Parentheses**: Evaluate expressions within parentheses first. If there are nested parentheses, start with the innermost ones and work your way out.

    1. Example: $2 \times (3 + 4) = 2 \times 7 = 14$

- **Exponents**: Evaluate expressions with exponents (powers and roots) next.

    1. Example: $2^3 + 4 = 8 + 4 = 12$

- **Multiplication and Division**: Perform multiplication and division from left to right.

    1. Example: $2 \times 3 + 4 = 6 + 4 = 10$

    2. Example: $6 \div 2 \times 3 = 3 \times 3 = 9$

- **Addition and Subtraction**: Perform addition and subtraction from left to right.

    1. Example: $2 + 3 \times 4 = 2 + 12 = 14$

    2. Example: $10 - 4 \div 2 = 10 - 2 = 8$

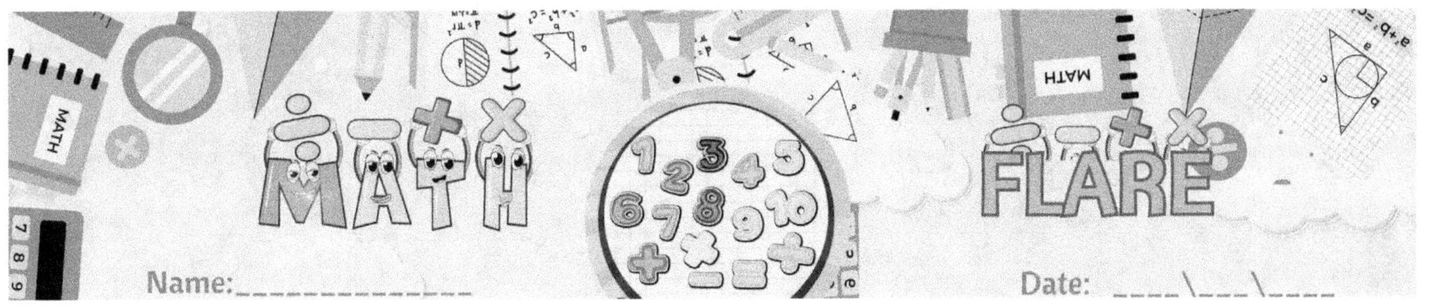

Positive and Negative Integers

Evaluate.

1. $(-11) - (-20) =$

2. $7 + 15 - (10 + 17) =$

3. $(-5) - 10 =$

4. $3 - (-1) - 7 =$

5. $15 + 17 - (6 + 2) =$

6. $(-20) + (-13) - 4 =$

7. $2 - 13 + 10 =$

8. $4 - (-1) =$

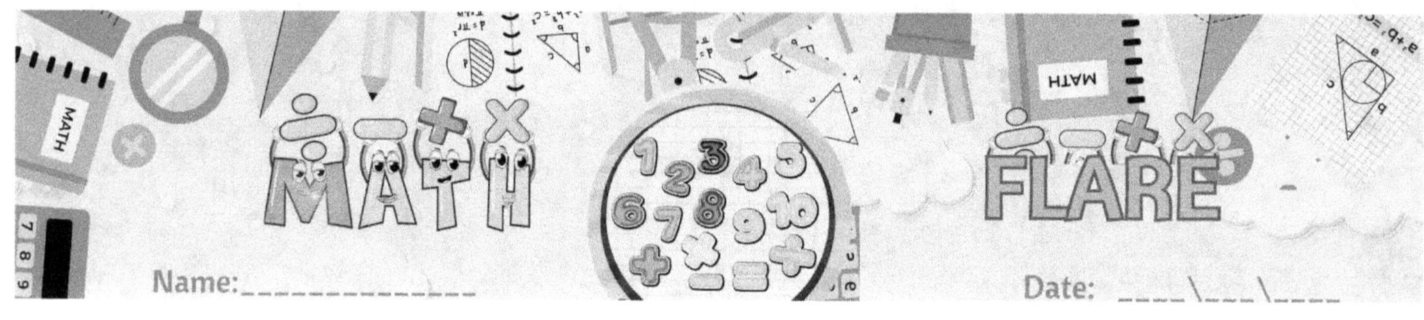

9. $(14 - 12) - (19 + 16) =$

10. $(-3) + (-12) + 14 =$

11. $(-12) + (-17) + 4 =$

12. $(-1) + (-7) =$

13. $(1 + 3) - (9 + 11) =$

14. $16 + (8 - 7) =$

15. $(-10) + 3 =$

16. $11 - (14 + 20) - 13 =$

17. $11 - 2 + (-20) =$

18. $(16 + 16) - 15 =$

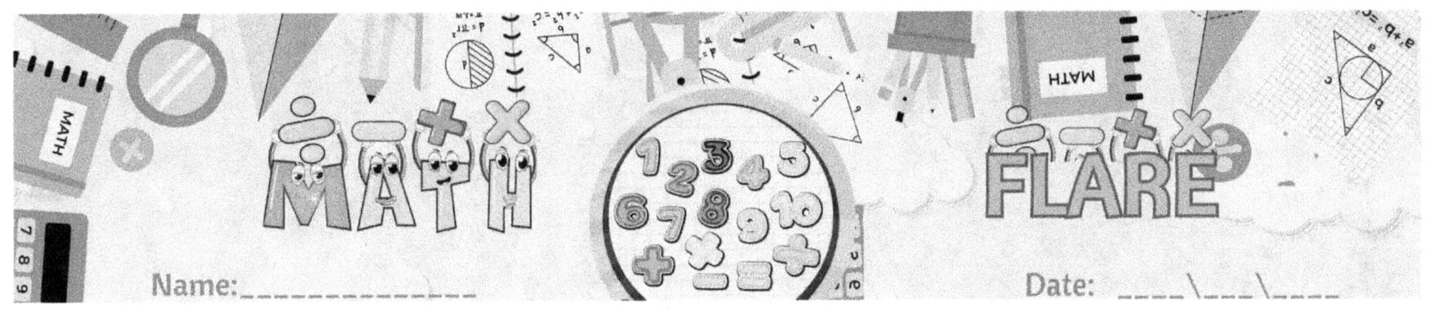

19. $7 - (7 + 19) + 13 =$

20. $(-3) - (-11) + 1 =$

21. $2 - 18 + 10 =$

22. $9 - 10 - 11 - 16 =$

23. $(20 - 2) - 18 =$

24. $(5 - 13) - (6 - 5) =$

25. $3 - 15 - (18 + 3) =$

26. $(-19) - (-20) - (-4) =$

27. $12 - 10 + 14 =$

28. $16 + (2 - 9) =$

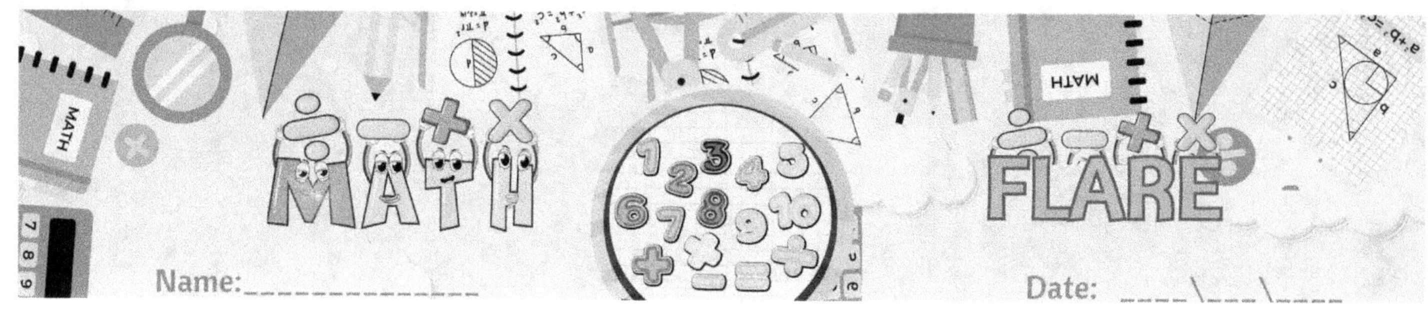

29. $(-15) + (-1) + 3 =$

30. $(-10) - (-6) + 1 =$

31. $(-16) - (-6) + 10 =$

32. $20 + (-14) =$

33. $(-2) + (-3) - 4 =$

34. $14 + (-10) - 5 =$

35. $15 - (3 + 10) - 10 =$

36. $4 - (12 + 1) - 11 =$

37. $(-5) - (-11) + 18 =$

38. $11 + 9 - 17 + 14 =$

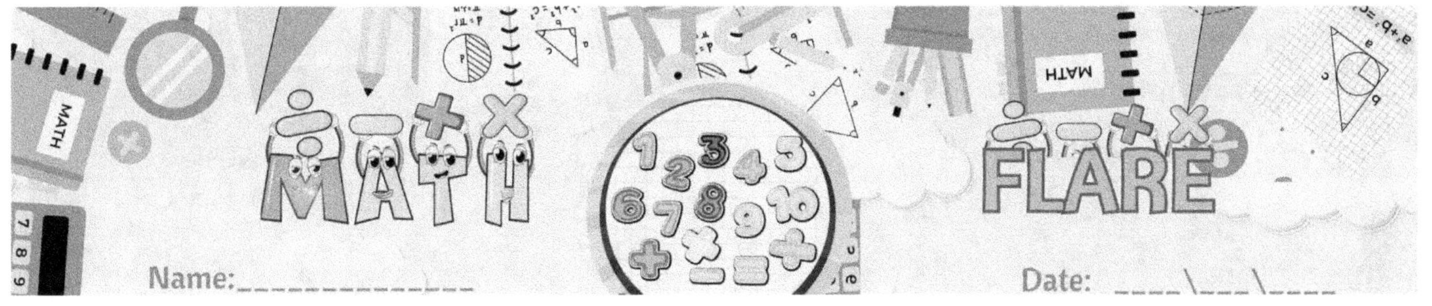

39. $(9 + 3) - 1 =$

40. $(-20) - (-19) + 8 =$

41. $20 + 13 - 11 =$

42. $(-20) - (-14) + 16 =$

43. $(5 + 1) - (17 + 16) =$

44. $11 + 3 - (5 + 20) =$

45. $(-13) + (-12) + (-19) =$

46. $(12 - 9) - (2 - 19) =$

47. $2 - 10 + 18 =$

48. $16 - (1 + 3) - 1 =$

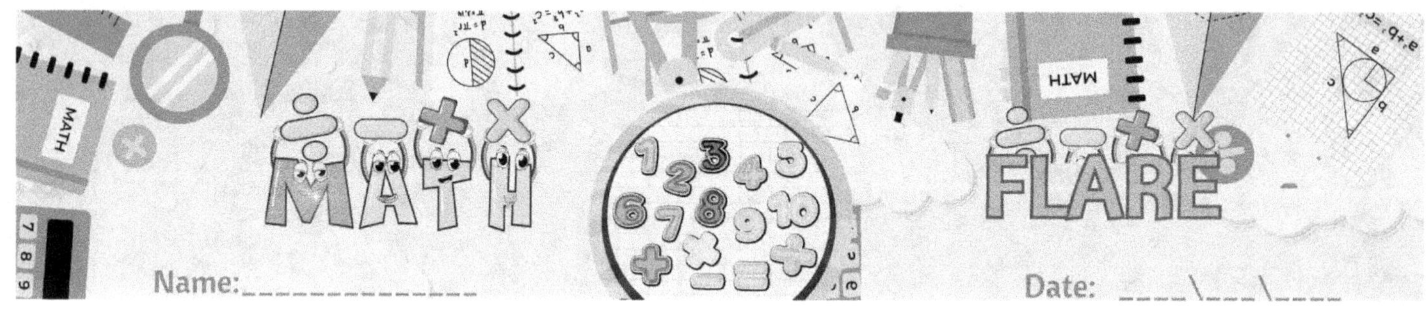

49. $(-14) - 1 =$

50. $4 - 15 - 11 =$

51. $17 - 15 + 11 =$

52. $20 - (11 + 11) - 17 =$

53. $(17 + 10) + 8 - 16 =$

54. $(-8) + (-8) + 4 =$

55. $17 - (-1) - 18 =$

56. $4 - (-9) =$

57. $11 - 18 - (9 + 19) =$

58. $4 - (13 + 5) - 13 =$

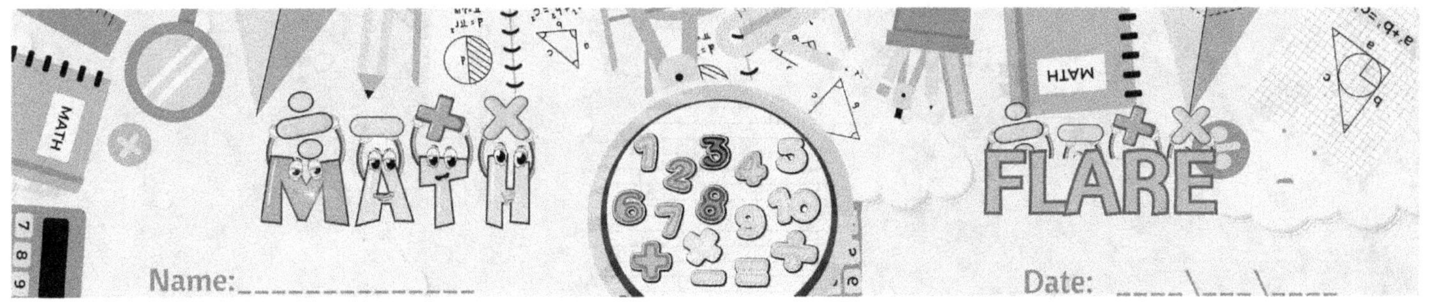

59. $13 - 4 + 8 =$

60. $16 - (-13) - 16 =$

61. $13 + 8 - 5 =$

62. $(3 + 12) - (9 - 2) =$

63. $12 - 6 - 10 =$

64. $14 + 14 - 11 =$

65. $(8 + 18) + (6 - 1) =$

66. $17 - (17 + 15) - 4 =$

67. $14 + (8 - 17) =$

68. $(-8) + 7 + (-6) =$

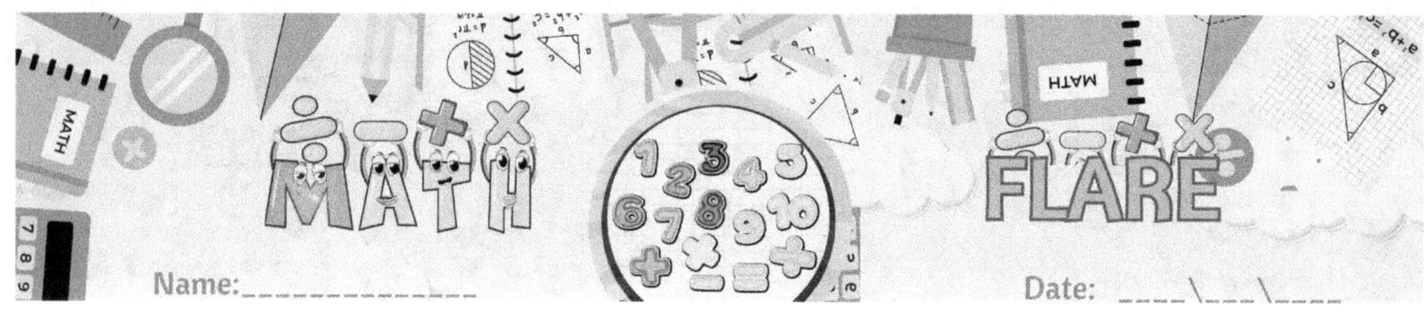

Name:________________

Date: _______________

69. $18 + 4 - 14 =$

70. $(-3) + 13 + (-4) =$

71. $(-12) + (-16) =$

72. $16 + (-13) - 18 =$

73. $6 - (15 + 8) - 20 =$

74. $12 + 20 - 5 =$

75. $(-10) - (-3) - (-17) =$

76. $(16 + 7) + 3 - 12 =$

77. $(-19) + 18 + (-13) =$

78. $(-20) + (-20) + 8 =$

79. $(16 + 6) + 4 - 5 =$

80. $(-8) + (-13) + (-7) =$

81. $(2 - 11) - (19 - 13) =$

82. $2 - 14 - (4 + 12) =$

83. $(-3) + 8 + (-5) =$

84. $(2 + 9) - (12 - 18) =$

85. $4 - 9 + 3 =$

86. $(18 - 11) - (12 + 14) =$

87. $(-6) - 20 =$

88. $17 - (-16) - 6 =$

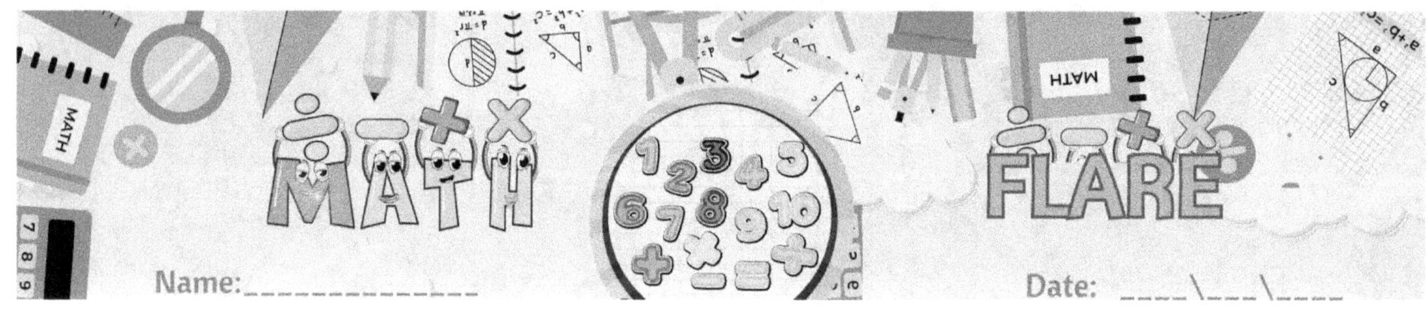

89. $(-2) + 20 =$

90. $(-12) + 4 + (-12) =$

91. $(-20) + (-13) + (-4) =$

92. $(19 - 5) - (5 + 14) =$

93. $14 - 20 - 20 =$

94. $17 - 11 + (-9) =$

95. $(-18) - (-12) - (-16) =$

96. $(-18) + 2 =$

97. $(-15) - (-2) =$

98. $(-11) - (-2) - (-16) =$

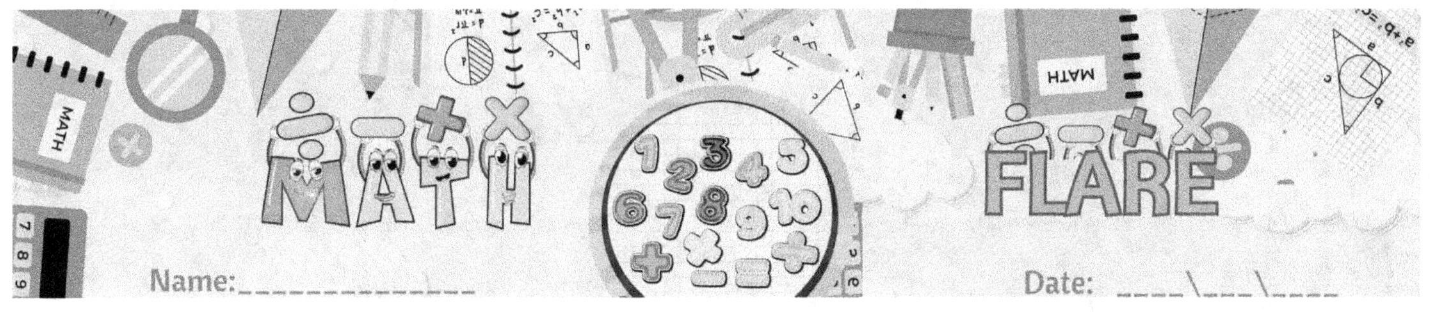

99. $(-9) + (-5) + (-20) =$

100. $(-17) + (-6) + 9 =$

101. $2 - 12 - 11 =$

102. $4 - 13 + 2 =$

103. $(-16) - (-9) + 19 =$

104. $20 - 5 + (-9) =$

105. $(-4) + 12 + (-12) =$

106. $(17 + 16) - (11 + 19) =$

107. $(5 + 10) - 4 =$

108. $(-19) - (-18) - (-2) =$

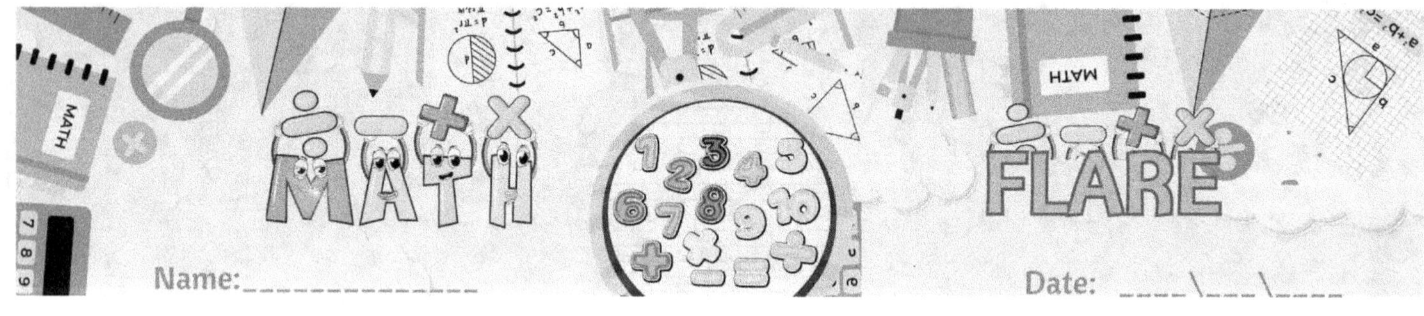

109. $1 - (19 - 18) =$

110. $(16 - 15) + (5 + 8) =$

111. $(-9) + 6 =$

112. $18 - (9 - 7) =$

113. $7 - (16 - 17) =$

114. $(-17) - 8 =$

115. $20 + (-2) - 10 =$

116. $14 + (-7) =$

117. $11 + 5 - (13 + 10) =$

118. $9 - (-19) - 2 =$

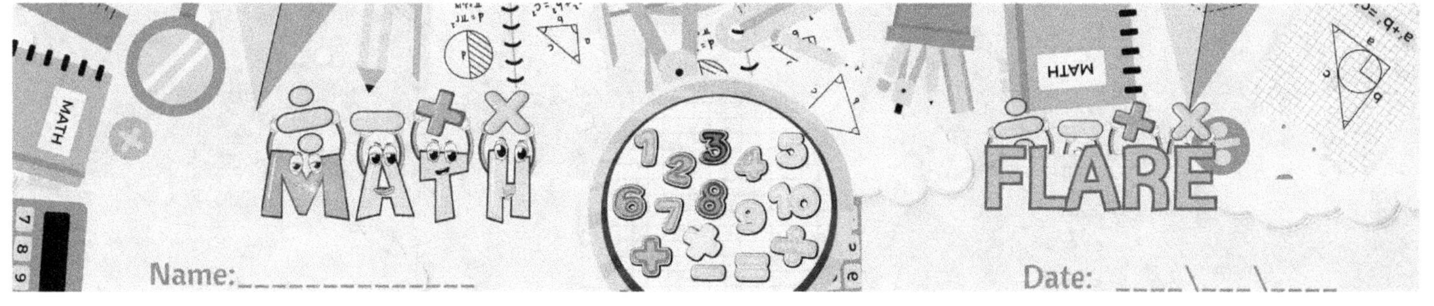

119. $(-14) + 3 + (-13) =$

120. $(4 - 19) + 14 - 5 =$

121. $16 + (17 - 1) =$

122. $19 - 14 - 3 =$

123. $11 + 10 - 16 =$

124. $(3 + 8) - (3 - 5) =$

125. $(-17) + (-8) + 8 =$

126. $15 + (-8) =$

127. $(-13) - (-4) - (-5) =$

128. $(16 - 10) - 7 =$

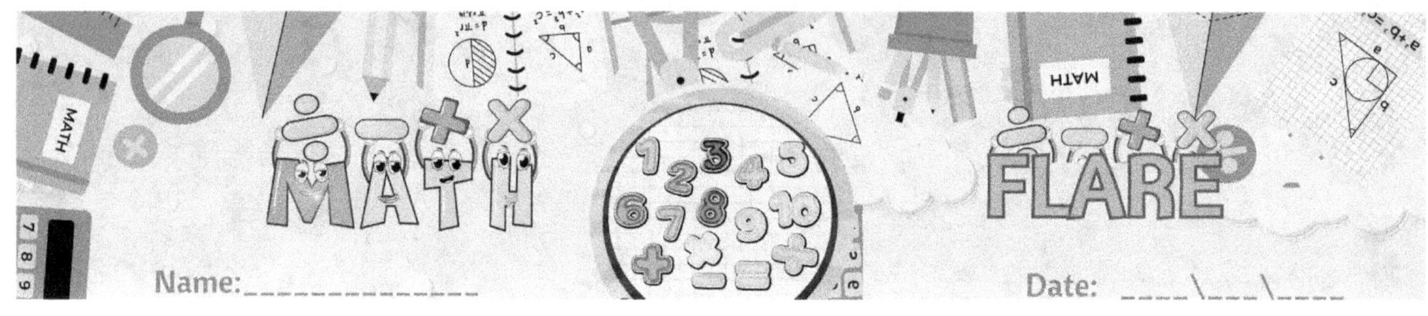

129. $7 + (-1) + 17 =$

130. $13 + (-4) =$

131. $4 - 14 + 19 =$

132. $15 - 15 - (7 + 14) =$

133. $14 - 8 + 17 =$

134. $(3 - 3) + (1 + 14) =$

135. $(17 + 14) - (17 - 13) =$

136. $16 + (6 - 15) =$

137. $(-18) - 16 + (-6) =$

138. $10 - (20 + 20) - 8 =$

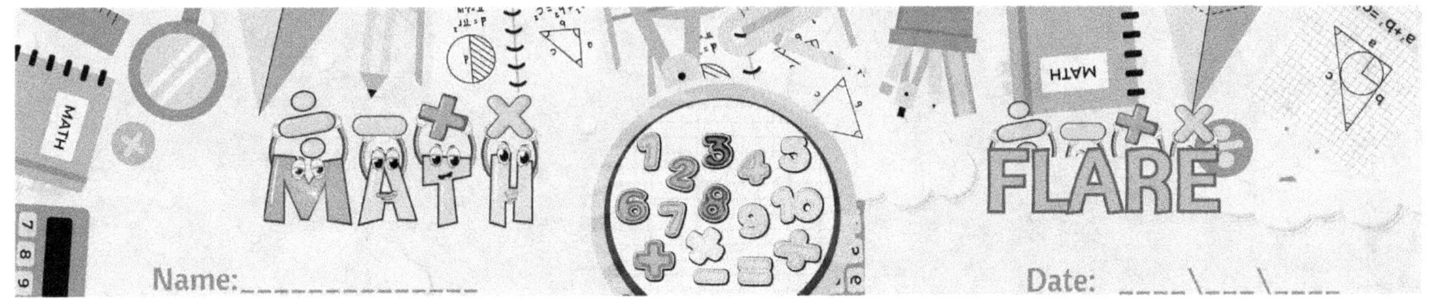

139. $14 + 12 - (14 + 7) =$

140. $18 + (-6) - 13 =$

141. $(-9) - 10 =$

142. $(-8) + (-11) + 11 =$

143. $15 - (15 + 7) - 12 =$

144. $11 + (-2) - 5 =$

145. $3 + 14 - 13 =$

146. $(-11) - (-8) =$

147. $1 + (-8) =$

148. $(10 + 6) - (18 - 13) =$

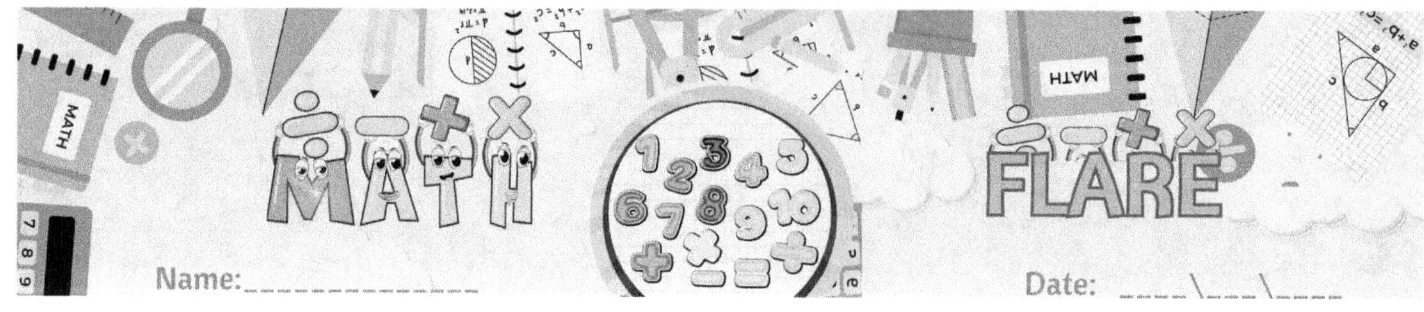

149. $5 + 15 - (7 + 6) =$

150. $(-20) + 17 =$

151. $(-4) - (-16) + 5 =$

152. $15 - 1 - (8 + 4) =$

153. $(-9) + (-3) + 6 =$

154. $(-12) - 20 + (-12) =$

155. $(-5) - (-16) + 9 =$

156. $15 - (17 + 14) - 1 =$

157. $2 - 6 + (-7) =$

158. $(10 - 16) + (8 + 12) =$

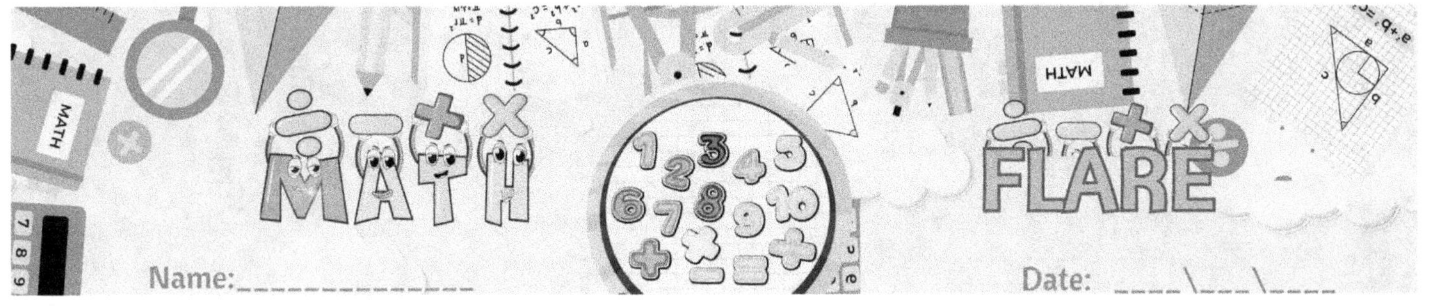

159. $(-18) + (-4) + 16 =$

160. $(-4) + (-9) + (-16) =$

161. $11 + 8 - 15 =$

162. $17 - (10 + 3) + 7 =$

163. $9 + (-2) + 6 =$

164. $15 + 16 - 10 + 14 =$

165. $(-14) + 18 =$

166. $16 - 1 + 11 =$

167. $(13 - 19) - 15 =$

168. $(-18) + 10 =$

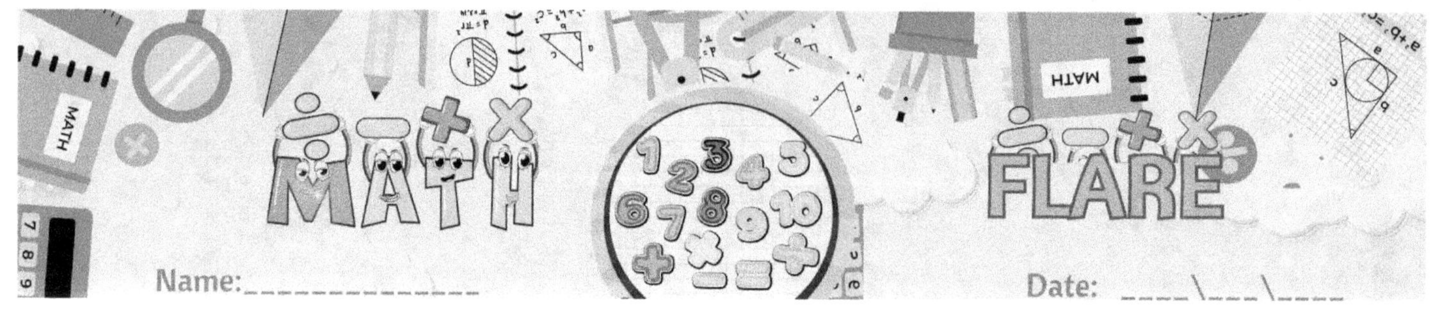

169. $16 + (-20) - 14 =$

170. $(16 - 7) - (5 + 7) =$

171. $(2 + 4) - (5 + 2) =$

172. $17 + 1 - (13 + 5) =$

173. $15 + 8 - 12 + 20 =$

174. $(1 - 12) + 15 - 7 =$

175. $(-14) - (-18) =$

176. $(-20) - (-9) + 16 =$

177. $14 + 17 - 17 + 16 =$

178. $11 + (-5) - 2 =$

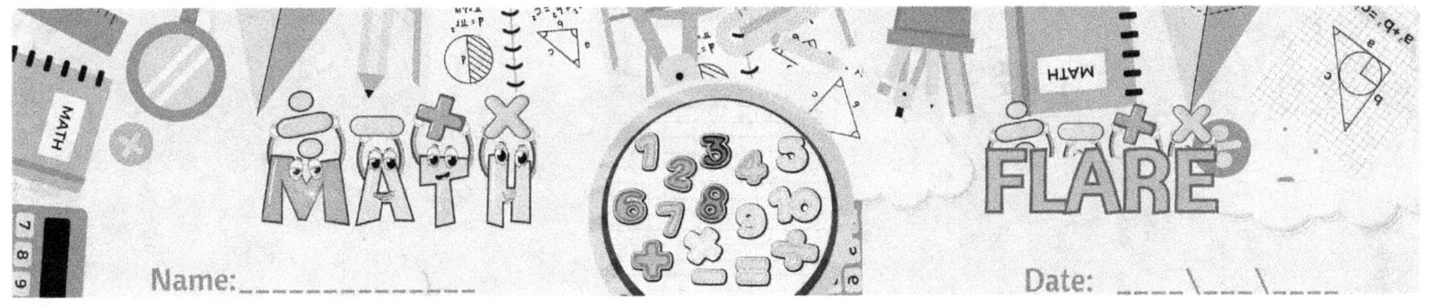

179. 11 – (9 – 11) =

180. (3 – 17) – (19 – 14) =

181. 13 – (5 + 13) – 18 =

182. 18 – 3 + 16 =

183. 16 + (– 5) =

184. 8 – (16 + 17) – 19 =

185. (1 + 13) + (1 – 19) =

186. (8 + 17) – 12 =

187. (9 – 8) – 9 =

188. (7 + 7) + (16 – 12) =

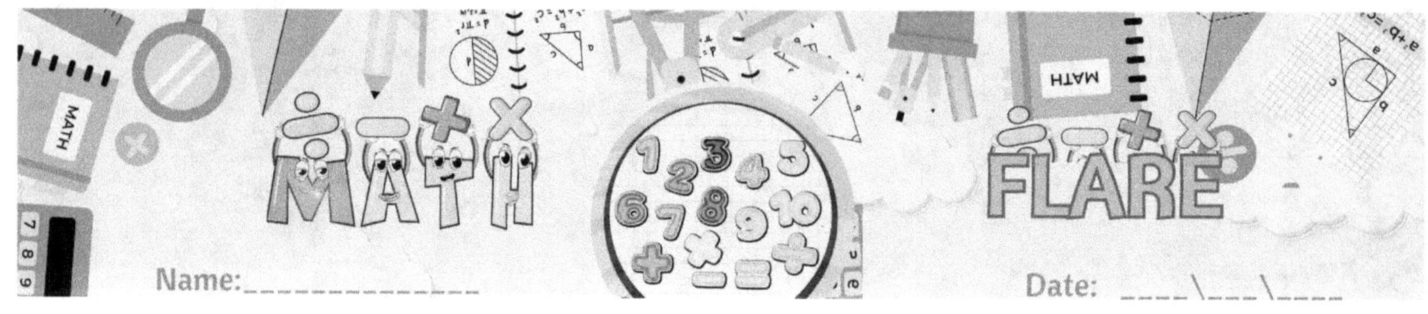

189. $14 + (-6) + 18 =$

190. $(10 + 3) - (3 - 18) =$

191. $3 - (-2) - 1 =$

192. $(1 - 3) - 6 =$

193. $1 - 18 - (12 + 9) =$

194. $20 + (14 - 7) =$

195. $(-1) + (-19) + 9 =$

196. $(12 + 15) + (1 - 7) =$

197. $(6 - 6) - (17 + 7) =$

198. $(12 + 2) - (12 - 2) =$

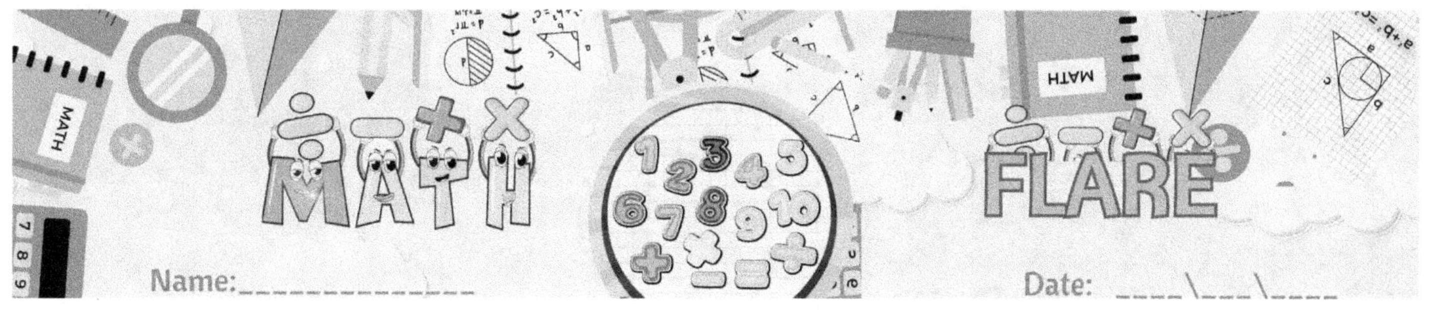

199. $11 - (-8) =$

200. $18 - (14 + 15) + 1 =$

201. $(-3) - 9 + (-20) =$

202. $(-12) - (-6) =$

203. $(9 + 12) - (19 + 6) =$

204. $18 - (-12) =$

205. $(2 - 17) - 6 =$

206. $14 + 14 - 10 =$

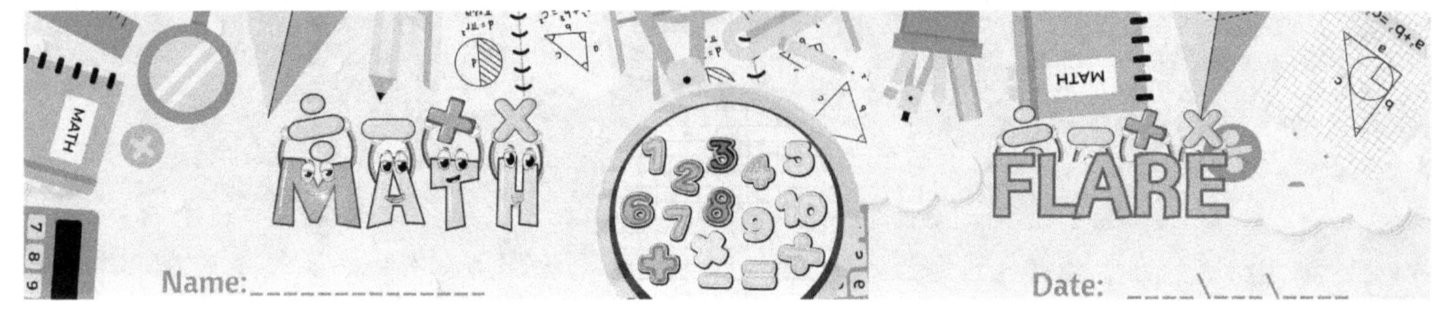

207. $(-17) - 16 =$

208. $(-3) + 19 =$

209. $9 + (4 - 19) =$

210. $(-16) + 17 + (-13) =$

211. $(13 - 18) + (15 + 17) =$

212. $(-18) + 1 =$

213. $6 + 17 - 11 =$

214. $(-6) - 1 + (-5) =$

215. $20 + 18 - 16 + 19 =$

216. $(-14) + (-18) + (-8) =$

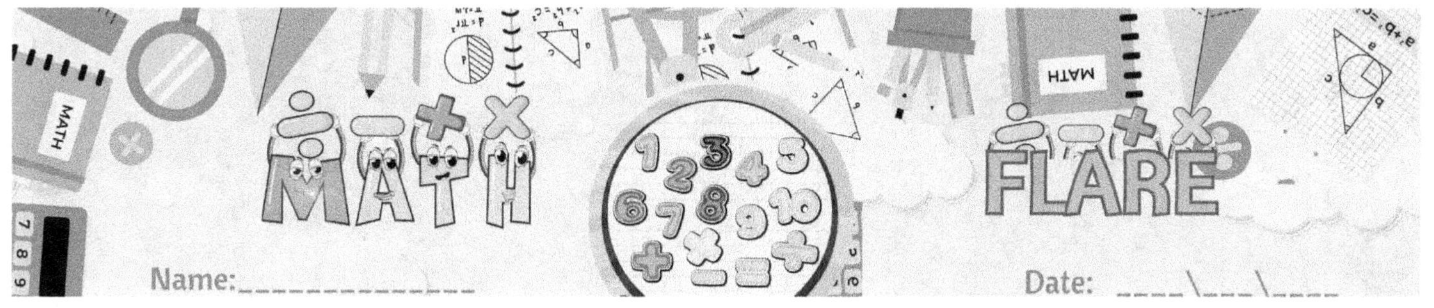

217. $(-18) - (-3) + 5 =$

218. $(3 + 4) - 1 - 9 =$

219. $1 + (-7) - 15 =$

220. $(-6) + (-1) + (-17) =$

221. $(-9) + (-16) =$

222. $(20 + 2) - 12 + 2 =$

223. $15 + (-1) =$

224. $(11 + 9) - 3 =$

225. $9 - (9 + 13) - 16 =$

226. $(-5) + (-4) =$

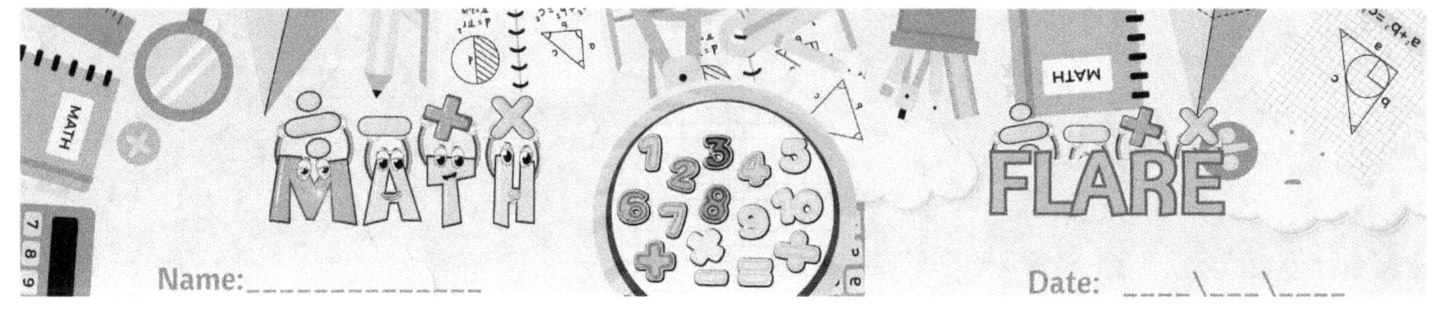

227. $10 + 11 - (1 + 8) =$

228. $19 - 10 - 8 =$

229. $(-15) + (-11) - 16 =$

230. $9 + 20 - 20 =$

231. $3 - 6 + 5 =$

232. $4 + 16 - (5 + 19) =$

233. $(-14) + 8 =$

234. $12 - 4 - (8 + 8) =$

235. $(-15) - 2 =$

236. $15 - 16 + 9 =$

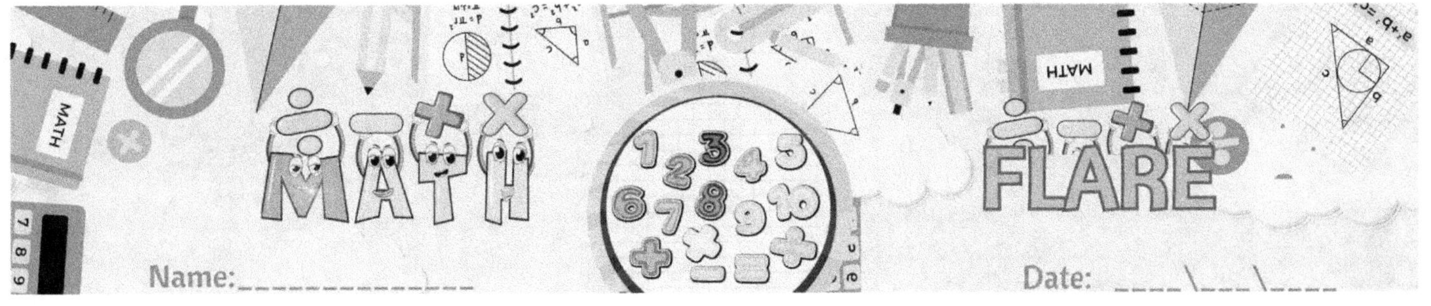

237. $13 - 17 + 4 =$

238. $(6 + 15) + 1 - 10 =$

239. $10 + (7 - 12) =$

240. $7 + (- 2) =$

241. $7 + 6 - 1 =$

242. $12 - 7 - 18 =$

243. $4 - 5 - 17 - 12 =$

244. $7 - (10 + 3) - 19 =$

245. $17 - 1 - (12 + 16) =$

246. $6 + 1 - (15 + 8) =$

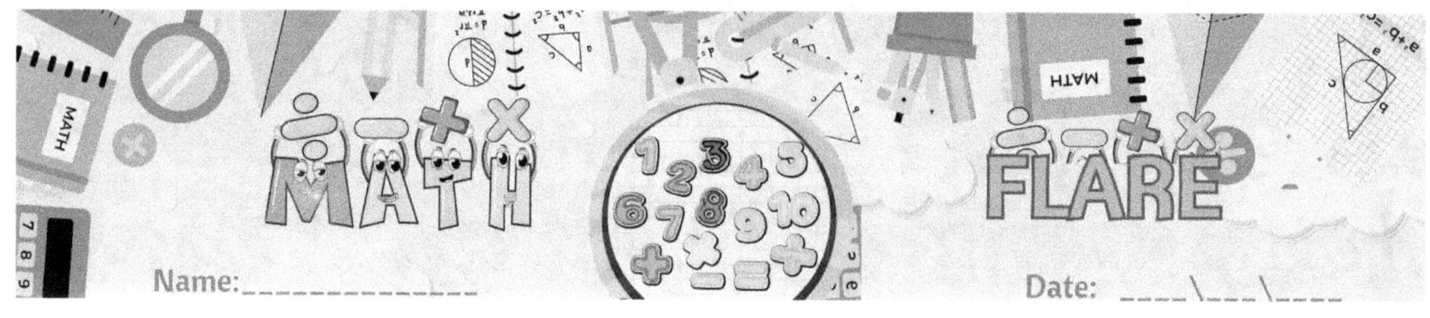

247. $17 - (-4) =$

248. $(17 + 18) + 11 - 4 =$

249. $(-15) - (-6) =$

250. $18 - (7 + 8) - 6 =$

251. $6 - 18 - 7 =$

252. $(-16) + (-9) + 5 =$

253. $11 - 11 + 12 =$

254. $2 - 11 + 14 =$

255. $4 + 17 - (4 + 9) =$

256. $(19 + 11) - 7 + 6 =$

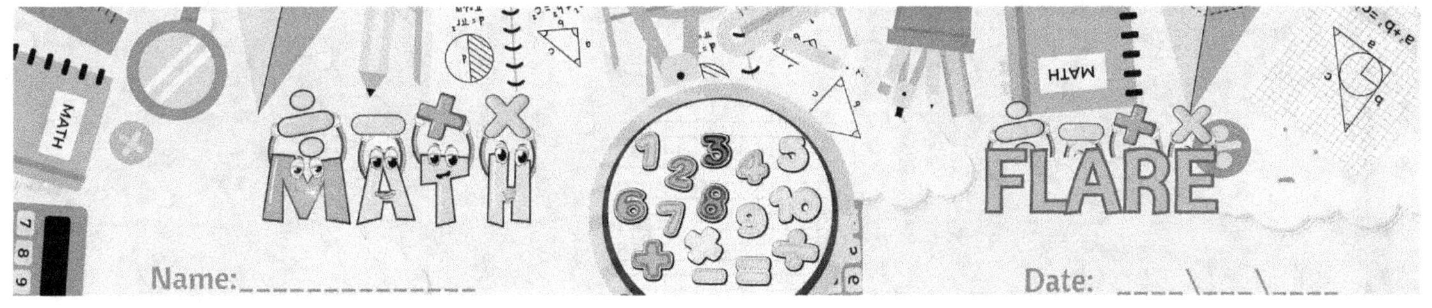

257. $(7 - 19) + 10 - 18 =$

258. $(-16) + 9 =$

259. $7 - 1 + 11 =$

260. $(11 + 14) - (20 + 3) =$

261. $(-17) - (-14) + 20 =$

262. $(15 - 16) + (8 + 1) =$

263. $11 - 5 + 16 =$

264. $16 + 13 - (3 + 15) =$

265. $15 - 20 - 6 =$

266. $(-8) + 7 + (-20) =$

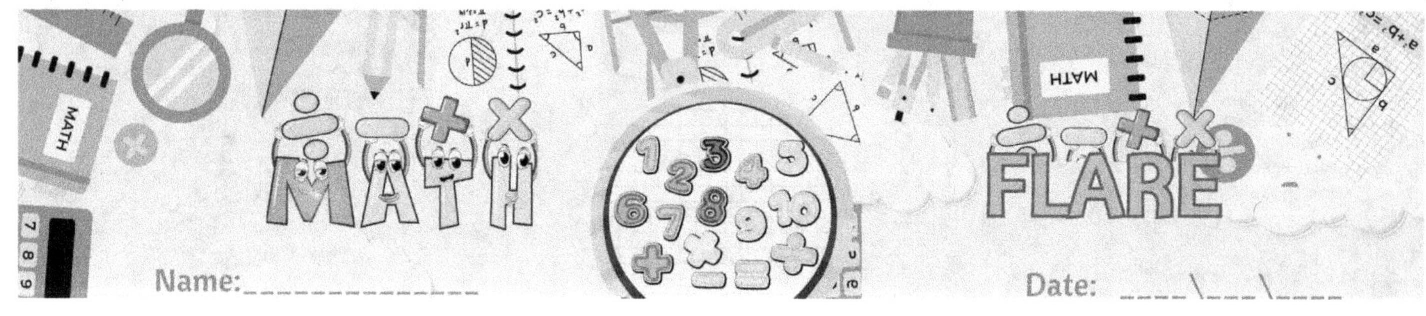

267. $2 - 19 + 7 =$

268. $8 + 9 - (1 + 20) =$

269. $19 - 10 + 1 =$

270. $1 - (8 + 11) - 11 =$

271. $7 - (-3) =$

272. $5 + (-15) - 3 =$

273. $(-4) - (-6) =$

274. $16 - (3 + 3) - 15 =$

275. $(5 + 13) - 15 =$

276. $(-13) - (-1) =$

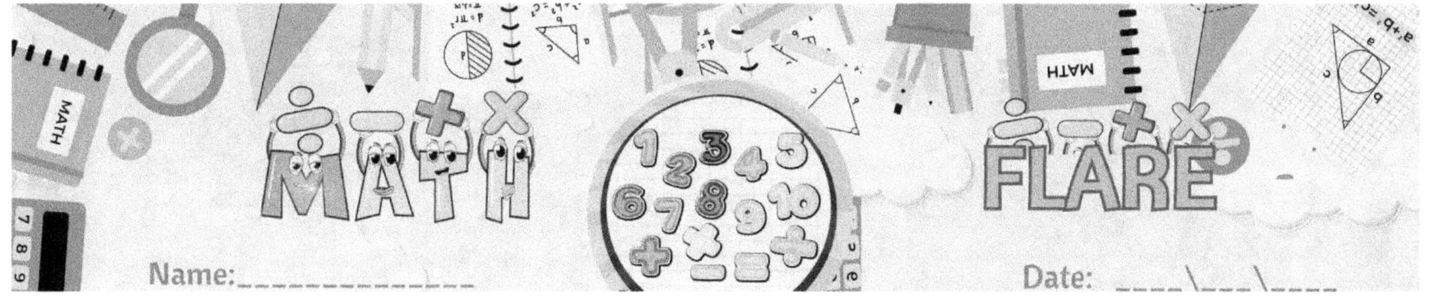

277. $5 - 4 + 7 =$

278. $1 - 2 - 19 - 8 =$

279. $12 - (6 + 16) + 8 =$

280. $3 - (-1) =$

281. $5 - 16 + (-8) =$

282. $(-3) - (-12) + 8 =$

283. $12 + 16 - 12 + 6 =$

284. $(4 + 14) + (7 - 16) =$

285. $4 - 14 + 5 =$

286. $9 + (-5) =$

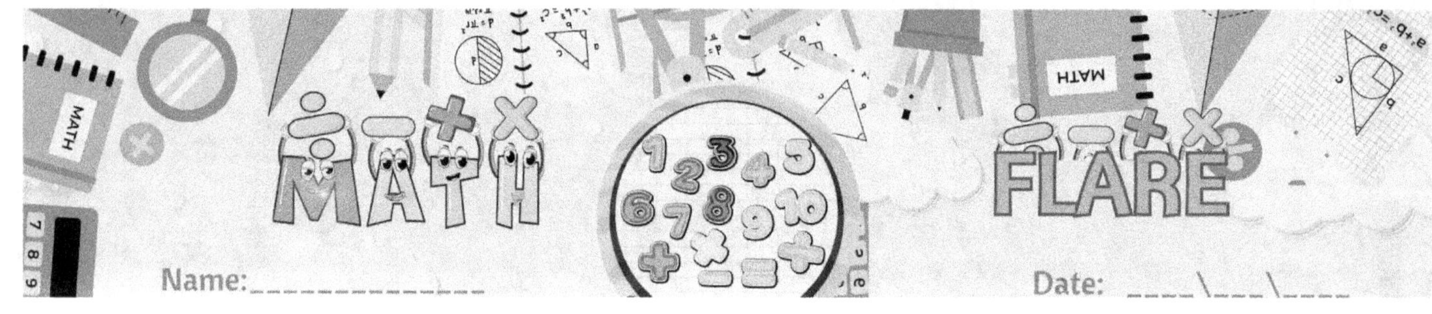

287. $(-6) - 10 + (-16) =$

288. $18 - (1 + 11) - 10 =$

289. $9 - (-16) - 13 =$

290. $(10 - 8) - (16 + 4) =$

291. $15 + (19 - 8) =$

292. $(-7) + (-3) + (-1) =$

293. $(-7) - (-1) =$

294. $6 - (13 + 19) + 4 =$

295. $7 + (16 - 3) =$

296. $4 + 19 - 2 =$

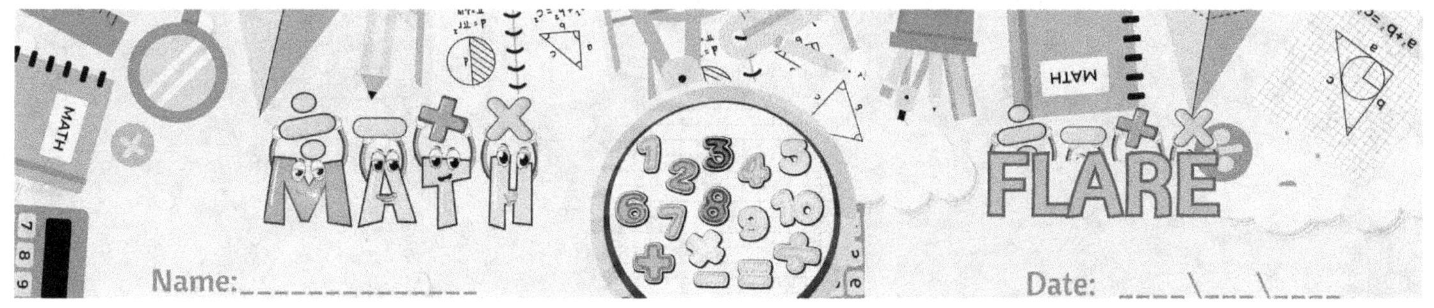

297. $(-7) + (-4) + (-17) =$

298. $(-12) + 9 + (-19) =$

299. $8 + (13 - 3) =$

300. $20 - (-17) =$

301. $3 + 3 - 18 =$

302. $8 + 11 - 12 + 18 =$

303. $(17 + 7) - (2 + 8) =$

304. $(18 - 6) - (4 - 4) =$

305. $19 + 17 - 4 =$

306. $(-14) + 6 =$

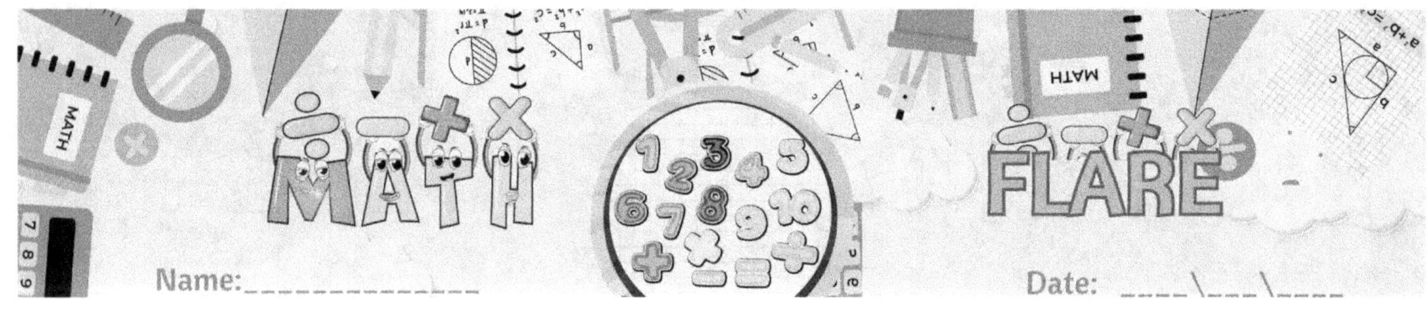

307. $13 - (-14) - 8 =$

308. $1 - (13 - 7) =$

309. $3 - 11 + 10 =$

310. $19 - (11 - 19) =$

311. $8 - 4 - 3 =$

312. $11 - 1 - 17 - 17 =$

313. $(4 - 5) - (7 + 13) =$

314. $(-20) + (-20) + 6 =$

315. $(-11) - (-9) + 6 =$

316. $(-20) + 11 =$

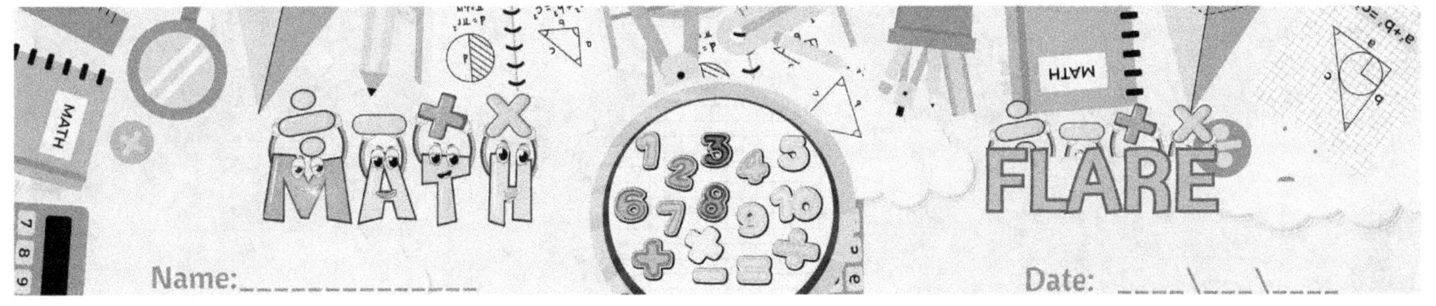

317. $9 + (-9) =$

318. $(14 - 5) + (10 + 15) =$

319. $18 - (-15) =$

320. $(4 + 10) + (8 - 8) =$

321. $8 + 12 - 10 =$

322. $(-11) + (-3) + 2 =$

323. $(13 + 19) - (1 - 8) =$

324. $(11 + 2) + (6 - 2) =$

325. $(-8) - 2 =$

326. $8 - 16 - 15 =$

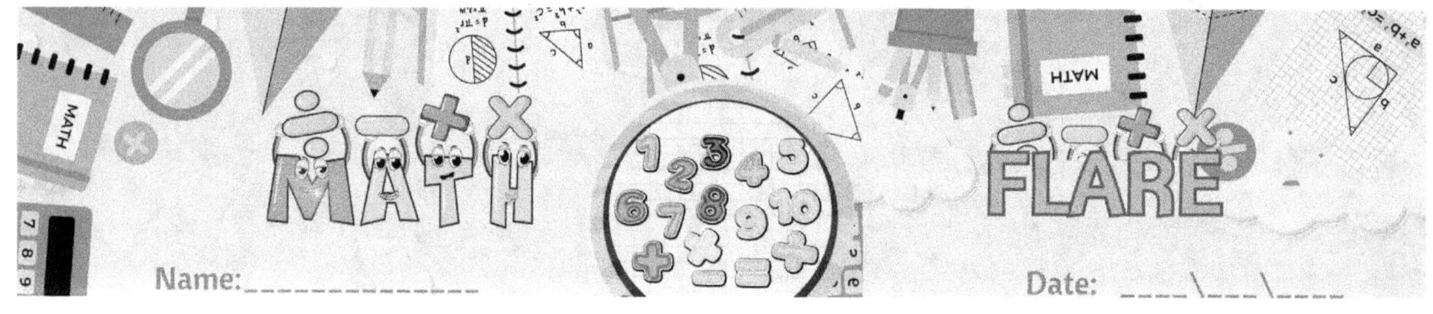

Name:________________   Date: ____________

327. $(6 + 10) - (9 - 2) =$

328. $(-10) - 14 + (-20) =$

329. $14 - (-16) =$

330. $3 + (-2) + 13 =$

331. $15 - 18 + (-19) =$

332. $5 + 9 - 10 + 15 =$

333. $(-9) + (-8) + 13 =$

334. $1 - 11 - 2 - 19 =$

335. $(13 - 19) - (8 - 7) =$

336. $17 + 8 - 8 =$

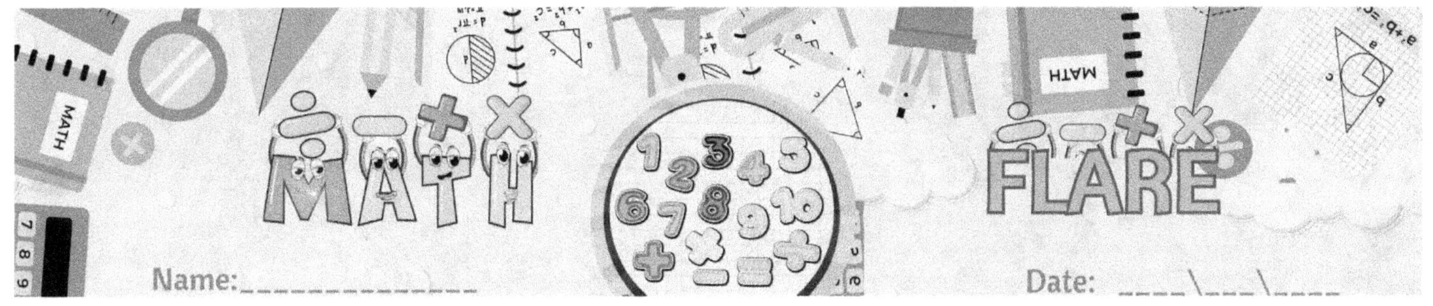

337. $15 + (-3) =$

338. $(-18) + 20 =$

339. $(11 + 1) - 18 =$

340. $3 + 8 - (18 + 16) =$

341. $20 - 15 - (16 + 4) =$

342. $8 + (-18) =$

343. $(-20) + 13 + (-14) =$

344. $7 + (-7) - 13 =$

345. $9 - 18 + (-1) =$

346. $12 - 2 + 2 =$

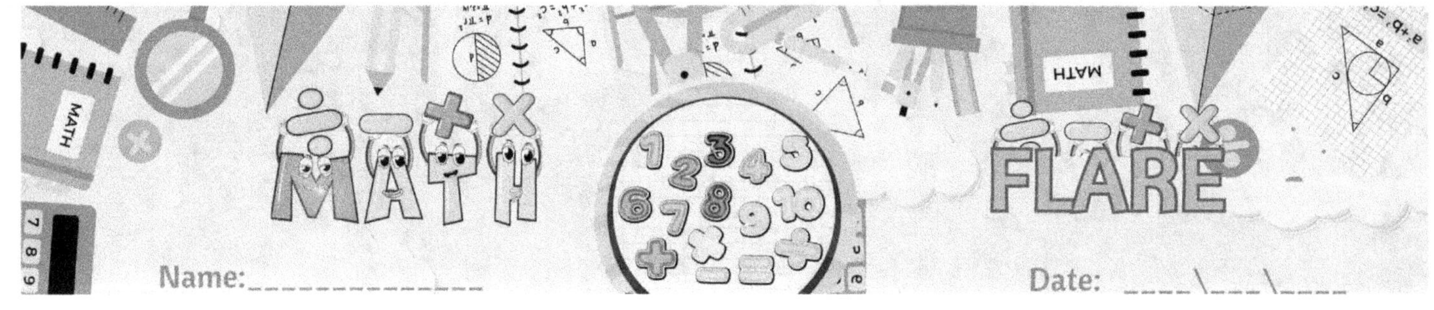

347. $(6 - 9) + 7 - 15 =$

348. $(-5) + 20 =$

349. $16 - 1 - (5 + 18) =$

350. $9 + 18 - 7 + 20 =$

351. $16 - (6 - 12) =$

352. $7 - (3 + 9) - 12 =$

353. $11 - (-7) - 4 =$

354. $14 - (1 + 9) - 10 =$

355. $(-10) - (-2) + 10 =$

356. $(10 - 16) - (2 + 3) =$

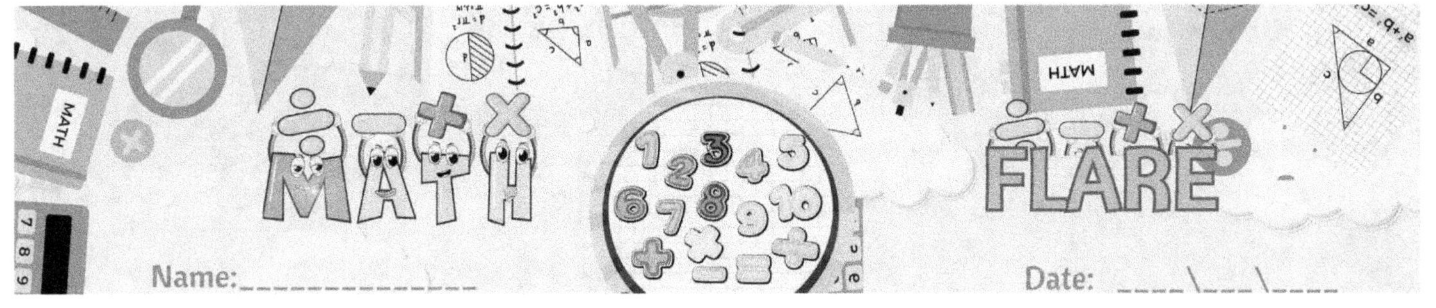

357. $9 - (-9) =$

358. $5 + (-11) =$

359. $17 + 9 - 7 =$

360. $(-13) - (-2) =$

361. $(4 + 16) - (1 - 8) =$

362. $(18 - 4) - (7 + 15) =$

363. $(9 + 13) - 11 + 15 =$

364. $2 + (-4) + 1 =$

365. $(4 + 12) + (6 - 12) =$

366. $(-3) - (-9) =$

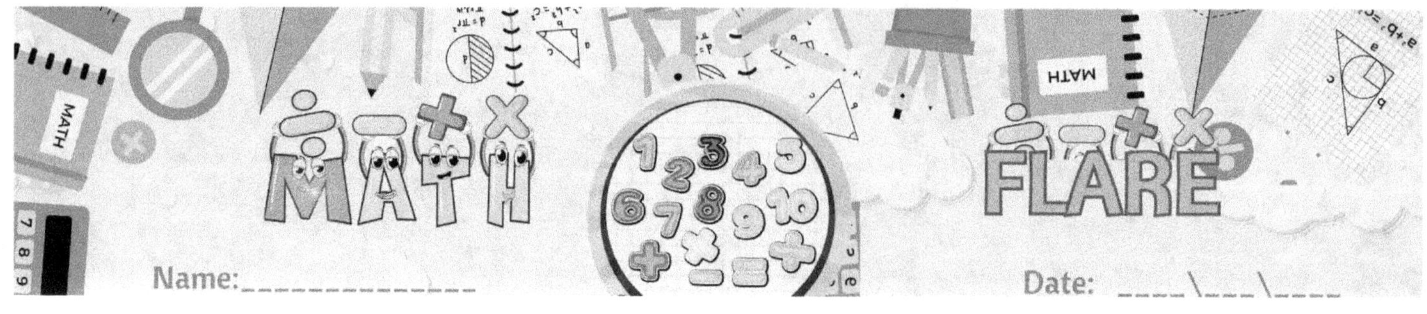

367. $20 - (2 - 5) =$

368. $17 + 7 - 18 =$

369. $7 - (17 - 7) =$

370. $1 - (5 + 18) - 6 =$

371. $(1 + 18) - 1 =$

372. $(1 + 13) - 6 + 16 =$

373. $(-16) + (-1) =$

374. $(-4) - (-12) =$

375. $(9 - 7) - (6 - 4) =$

376. $7 - (5 - 3) =$

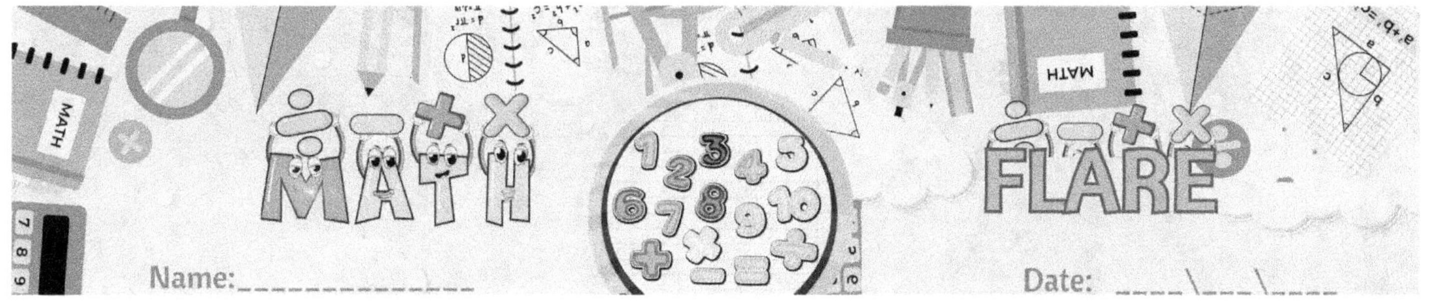

377. 15 − (11 − 14) =

378. (− 4) − (− 15) + 16 =

379. (12 − 11) − (7 + 20) =

380. (19 + 2) − (12 + 6) =

381. (18 − 17) + (3 + 3) =

382. 4 + 12 − 14 + 6 =

383. 7 + 14 − 19 =

384. 18 − (− 14) − 9 =

385. (1 + 12) − (3 − 11) =

386. 2 − (19 + 10) + 8 =

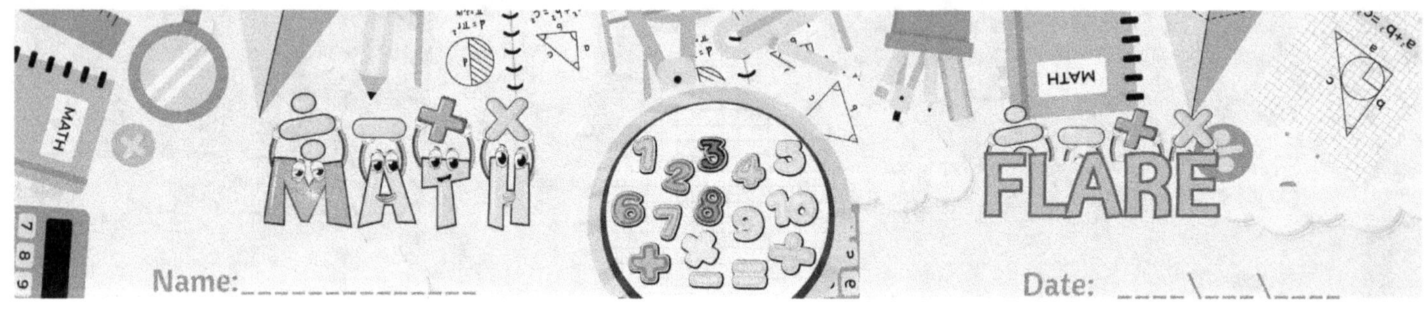

387. $(12 - 18) + 4 - 5 =$

388. $10 + 2 - (20 + 17) =$

389. $(17 + 19) + (13 - 6) =$

390. $12 - (11 + 3) - 2 =$

391. $3 - 14 + 9 =$

392. $9 + 4 - 1 + 5 =$

393. $17 - 2 - 3 - 11 =$

394. $(-15) - (-17) =$

395. $9 - 1 - 13 =$

396. $(-16) - 10 =$

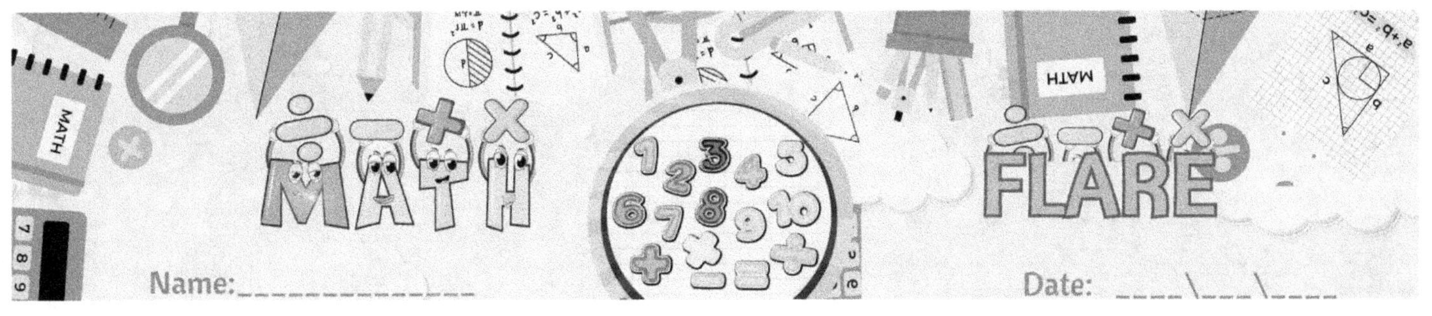

Order of Operations (PEMDAS)

Evaluate.

397. $1 \times 4 =$

398. $(4 + 7)^2 + (10 + 11)^2 =$

399. $4(16 + 15) =$

400. $(5 + 4)^2 =$

401. $(14^2) \times (9^2) + 3 =$

402. $(13^2) \times (14^2) + 14 =$

403. $(1^2) \times (9^2) + 12 =$

404. $9 + 4^2 + 7 + 10^2 =$

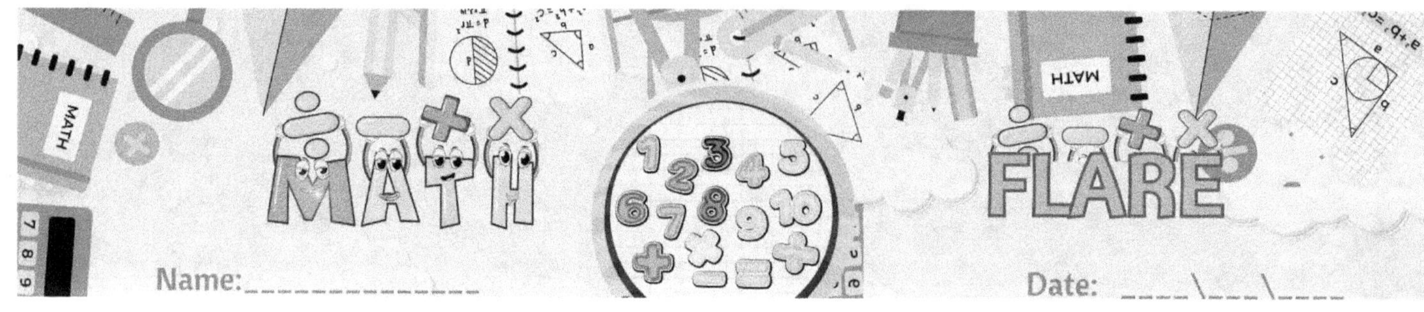

405. $(16 + 12)(5 + 2) =$

406. $19 \times 7 + 17 =$

407. $(3 + 6)^2 + (2 + 17)^2 =$

408. $3 + 7 + 4 + 14 =$

409. $(15 + 16) \div 10 =$

410. $4 + 7 + 12 =$

411. $(3 + 18) \times (10 + 6) =$

412. $14 \times (12 + 10) =$

413. $(16 + 19) \div 16 =$

414. $18 + 18 - 15 + 12 =$

415. $(18^2) \times (7^2) + 2 =$

416. $(17 \times 8) - (8 + 2) =$

417. $(8 + 7)(7 + 11) =$

418. $(8^2) \times (11^2) + 8 =$

419. $14 + 17 + 19 =$

420. $1 \times 1 =$

421. $(18^2) \times (13^2) + 15 =$

422. $(15^2) \times (17^2) + 5 =$

423. $(16^2) \times (7^2) + 7 =$

424. $(7 \times 6) - (19 + 6) =$

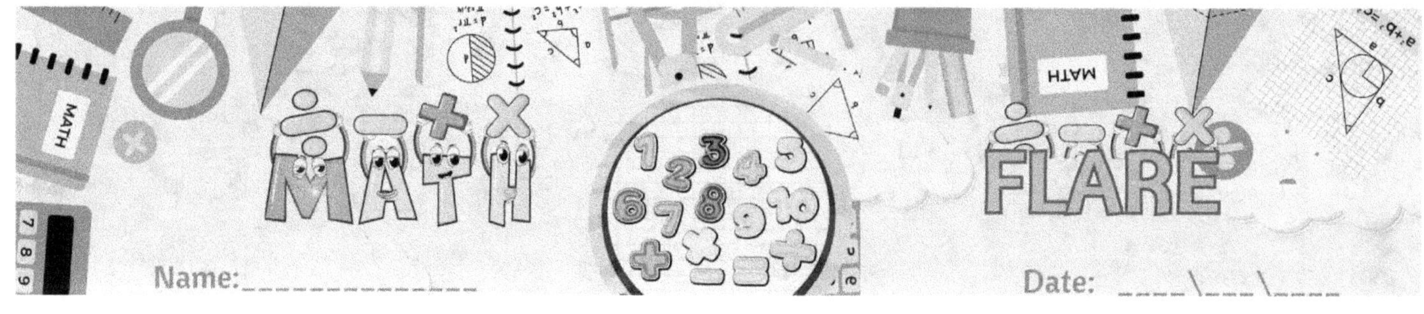

425. $12 + 13^2 + 16 + 8^2 =$

426. $14 \times 14 =$

427. $(16^2) \times (19^2) + 11 =$

428. $15 + 11 - 3 + 15 =$

429. $6 + 2 + 3 =$

430. $2 + 3 + 18 + 18 =$

431. $(17 + 17)^2 + (19 + 3)^2 =$

432. $12 \times 6 =$

433. $13 + 13 - 2 + 16 =$

434. $(1^2) \times (1^2) + 8 =$

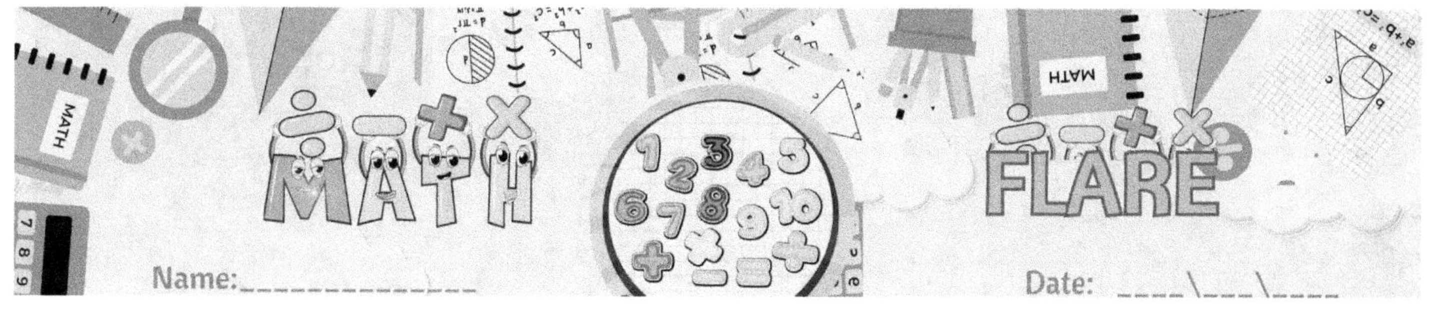

435. $(6^2) \times (17^2) + 18 =$

436. $(12^2) \times (7^2) + 3 =$

437. $6 \times (5 + 2) =$

438. $(8 + 19) \div 4 =$

439. $13 + 2 + 19 + 14 =$

440. $4 + 5 + 5 =$

441. $(9^2) \times (2^2) + 9 =$

442. $15(15 + 14) =$

443. $17 \times 9 + 1 =$

444. $(3 + 18)^2 + (15 + 14)^2 =$

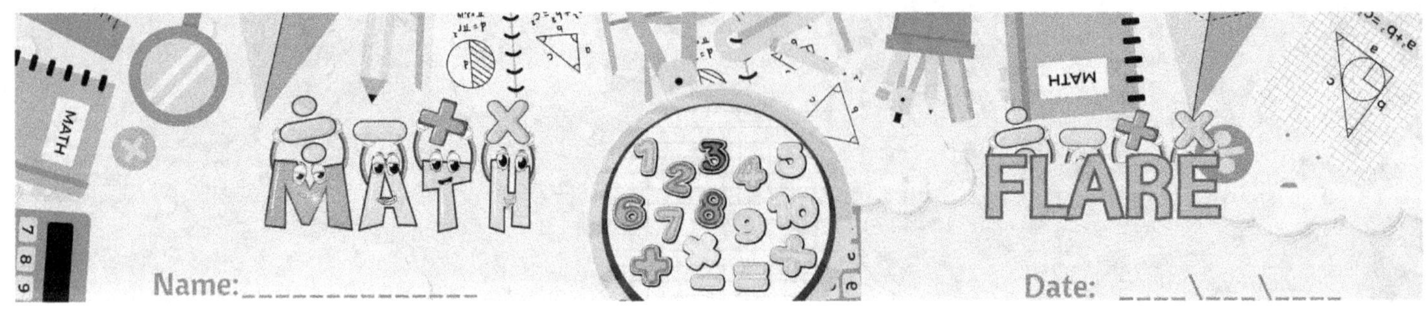

445. $(11^2) \times (16^2) + 10 =$

446. $10 + 4^2 + 12 + 16^2 =$

447. $20 + 13 - 13 + 16 =$

448. $10 + 1^2 + 19 + 20^2 =$

449. $4 + 14^2 =$

450. $20 + 18 + 11 =$

451. $17 \times 13 \times 7 =$

452. $(18 + 2)^2 + (4 + 19)^2 =$

453. $11 + 15^2 =$

454. $(5 \times 2) - (5 + 13) =$

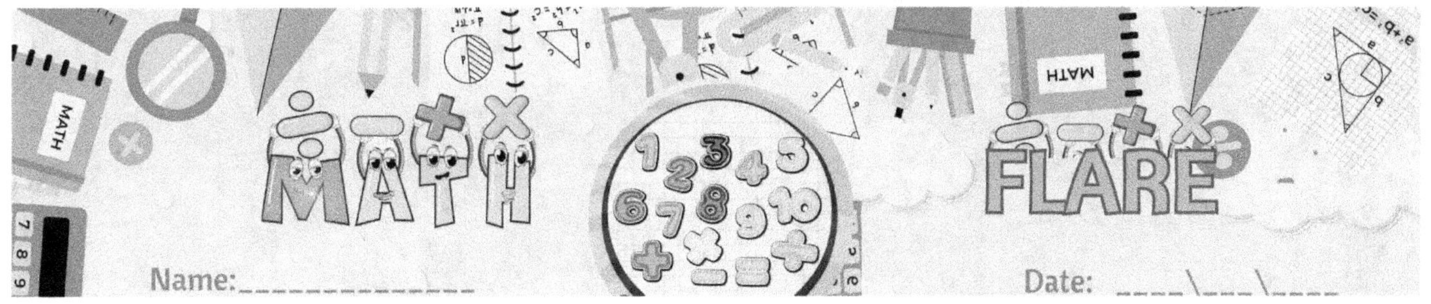

455. $(5 + 14)^2 + (17 + 13)^2 =$

456. $9 + 10 + 13 =$

457. $9(5 + 17) =$

458. $(9 + 14) \div 6 =$

459. $15 + 15 + 17 =$

460. $(5 + 8) \div 4 =$

461. $(1 + 5) \div 18 =$

462. $18 \times 10 =$

463. $12 + 9 + 1 + 13 =$

464. $6 \times (6 + 8) =$

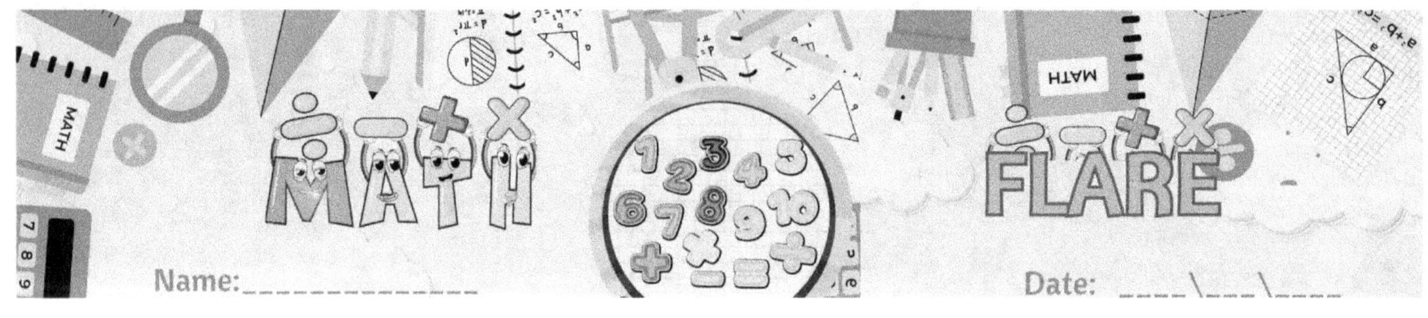

465. $(12 + 12) \div 17 =$

466. $(16^2) \times (5^2) + 3 =$

467. $12 + 5 + 10 + 5 =$

468. $2 + 13^2 =$

469. $(17 + 18) \div 5 =$

470. $17(10 + 5) =$

471. $14 + 11 - 18 + 19 =$

472. $4 + 9^2 =$

473. $8 \times 17 \times 8 =$

474. $1 + 1 + 10 =$

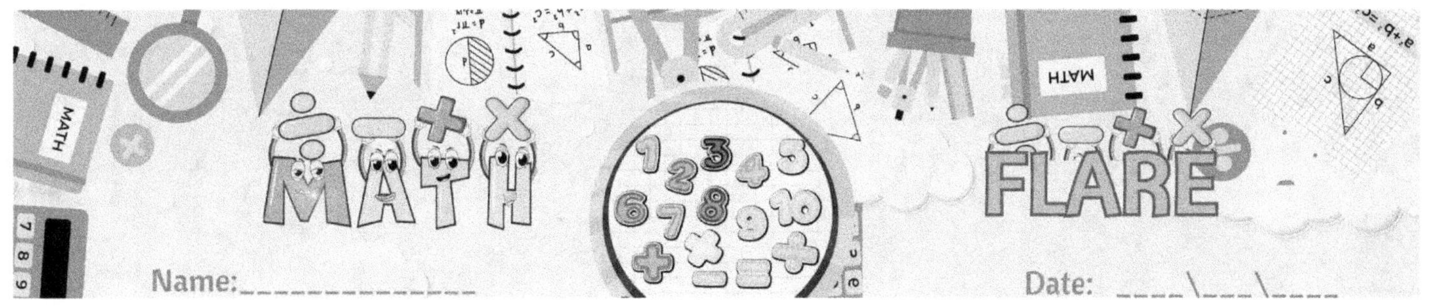

475. $20 + 4^2 + 20 + 9^2 =$

476. $(18^2) \times (3^2) + 9 =$

477. $(19 + 10)^2 =$

478. $15 + 13 + 3 =$

479. $(15 + 16)^2 =$

480. $3(5 + 2) =$

481. $(12 + 8) \times (12 + 12) =$

482. $9 + 13 - 15 + 11 =$

483. $(13 + 8)^2 =$

484. $(9^2) \times (9^2) + 9 =$

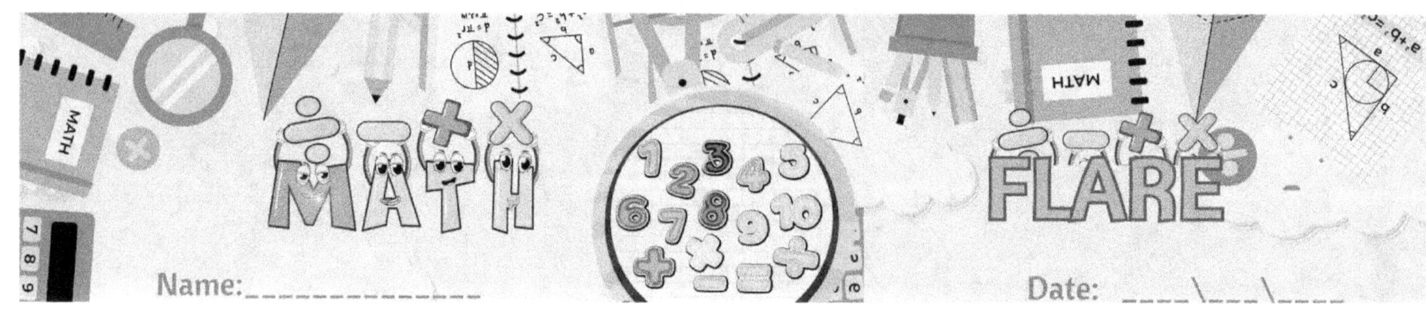

485. $(15 + 11) \times (4 + 1) =$

486. $5 + 19 + 14 =$

487. $(8 + 1)(2 + 9) =$

488. $(11 + 15)^2 + (20 + 18)^2 =$

489. $15 + 5 + 9 =$

490. $6 \times 3 \times 15 =$

491. $(17 + 14)(10 + 18) =$

492. $(12^2) \times (11^2) + 5 =$

493. $(19 + 5) \times (15 + 20) =$

494. $10 + 1^2 + 20 + 3^2 =$

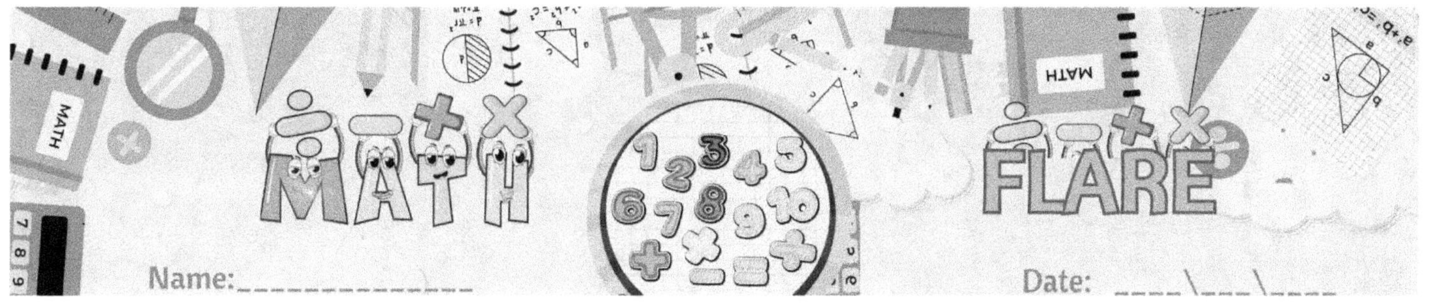

495. $(19 + 14)^2 + (12 + 5)^2 =$

496. $(12 + 15) \times (11 + 6) =$

497. $(4 + 1)(14 + 13) =$

498. $18(16 + 9) =$

499. $20 \times (4 + 7) =$

500. $15 + 18 + 18 =$

501. $15 + 3^2 =$

502. $(14 + 8)^2 =$

503. $9 \times (10 + 16) =$

504. $8 + 9^2 =$

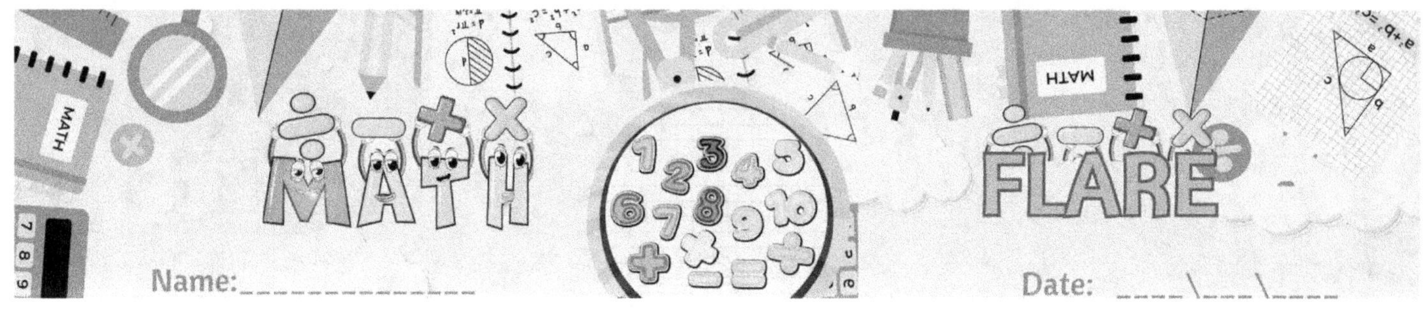

505. $2(15 + 20) =$

506. $15 \times 17 + 11 =$

507. $18(2 + 11) =$

508. $1 + 6^2 =$

509. $(8^2) \times (6^2) + 17 =$

510. $(18^2) \times (18^2) + 8 =$

511. $(3 \times 17) - (16 + 16) =$

512. $(3^2) \times (6^2) + 2 =$

513. $(6^2) \times (4^2) + 11 =$

514. $18 + 17 + 4 =$

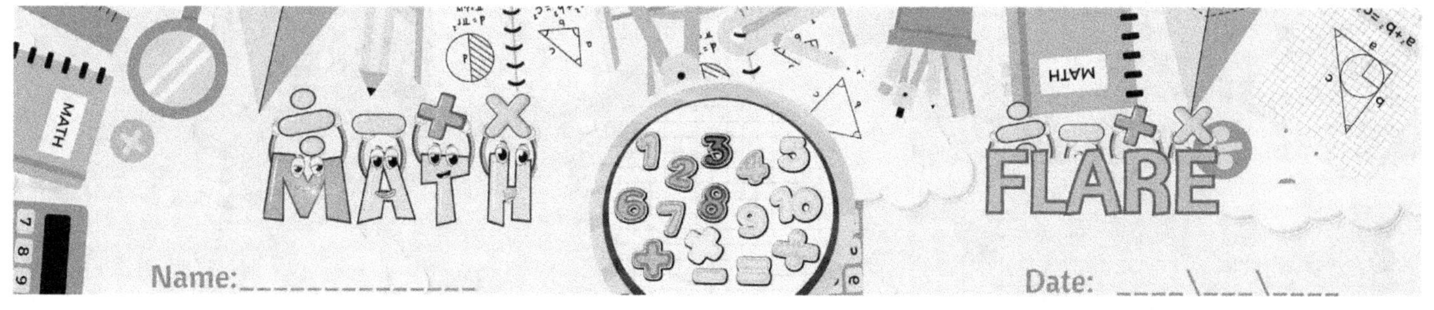

515. $5 + 16 + 19 + 15 =$

516. $20 + 20 - 14 + 3 =$

517. $(20^2) \times (19^2) + 3 =$

518. $3 + 17 - 15 + 13 =$

519. $11(10 + 7) =$

520. $(17 + 10) \times (1 + 8) =$

521. $(20^2) \times (12^2) + 14 =$

522. $(19 + 9) \div 19 =$

523. $(10 \times 13) - (20 + 20) =$

524. $(5 + 7)^2 =$

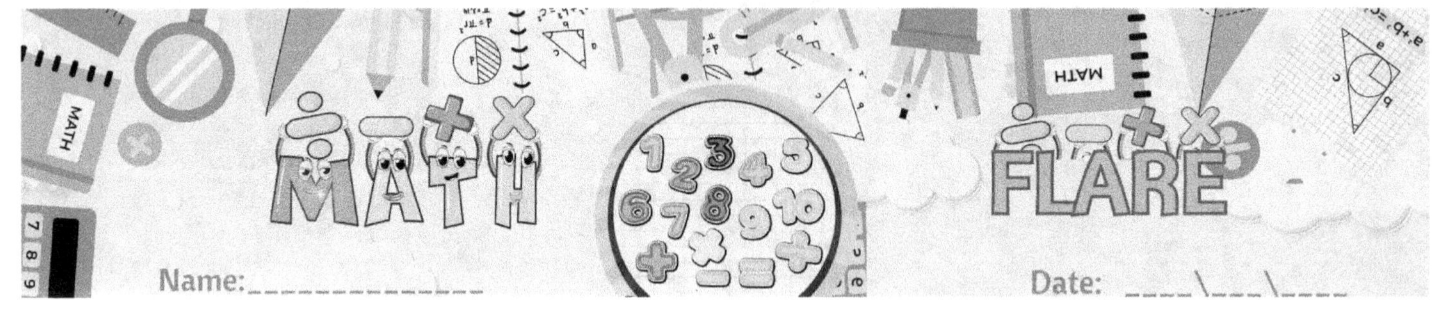

525. $16 + 11 + 9 + 11 =$

526. $18 \times (19 + 5) =$

527. $6 + 4 - 18 + 14 =$

528. $14 + 7 + 12 + 10 =$

529. $16 \times (15 + 5) =$

530. $2 \times (8 + 3) =$

531. $18(16 + 8) =$

532. $(2 + 1)^2 =$

533. $(11^2) \times (16^2) + 13 =$

534. $7 + 19^2 =$

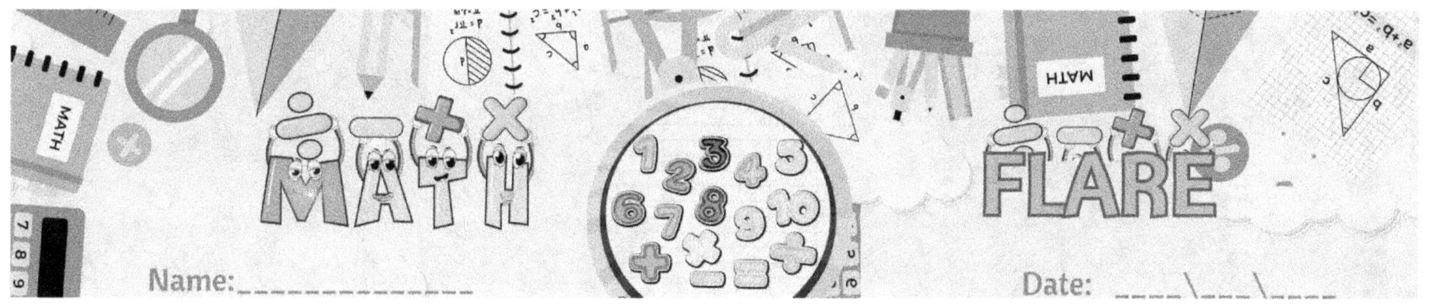

Name:_________________________ Date: _______________

535. $(3 \times 19) - (10 + 19) =$

536. $(2 + 2)^2 + (19 + 9)^2 =$

537. $(18^2) \times (5^2) + 16 =$

538. $4 + 2 + 18 + 20 =$

539. $(13^2) \times (17^2) + 9 =$

540. $14 + 19 + 16 + 18 =$

541. $18 + 5 + 18 + 16 =$

542. $(2 + 10) \div 18 =$

543. $(8^2) \times (10^2) + 13 =$

544. $17 \times (20 + 12) =$

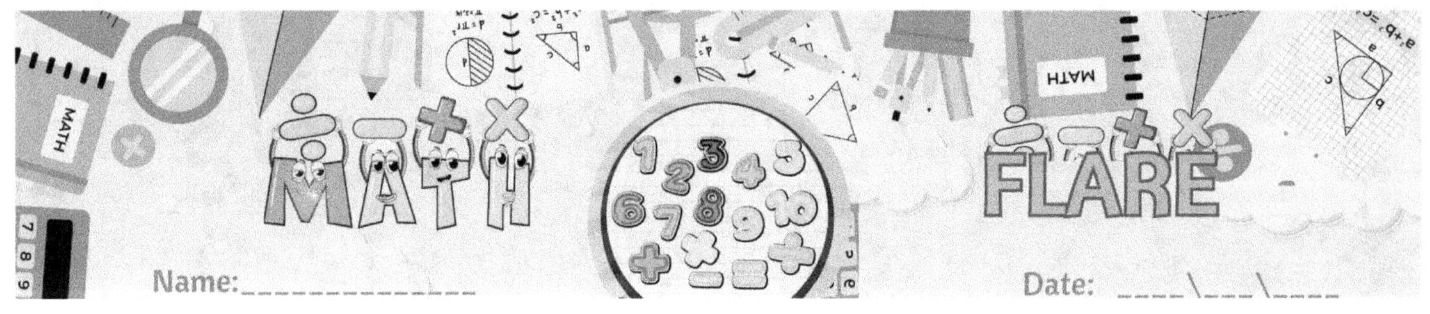

545. $(16 + 17) \times (14 + 8) =$

546. $14 + 16 + 17 =$

547. $4 + 3 + 8 =$

548. $(14 + 14) \times (10 + 2) =$

549. $8 + 14^2 =$

550. $7 \times 19 =$

551. $9 \times 4 =$

552. $(5 + 1)^2 + (6 + 1)^2 =$

553. $6 + 1 + 10 =$

554. $(11 + 10)(16 + 3) =$

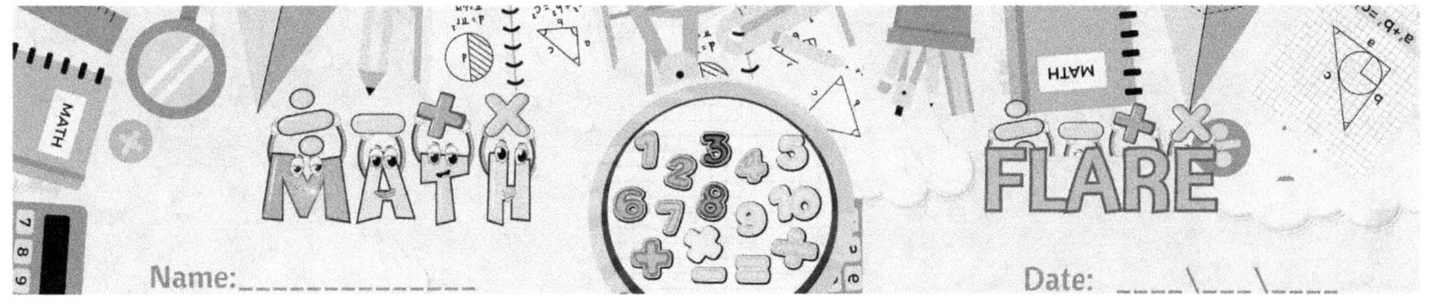

555. $8 + 3 - 7 + 5 =$

556. $16 + 4 - 1 + 1 =$

557. $3 + 19 - 14 + 16 =$

558. $17 + 4^2 + 3 + 12^2 =$

559. $8 \times 10 =$

560. $15 + 3^2 + 14 + 9^2 =$

561. $16 + 7 + 15 =$

562. $(12^2) \times (13^2) + 3 =$

563. $14 \times 7 + 6 =$

564. $14 + 7^2 =$

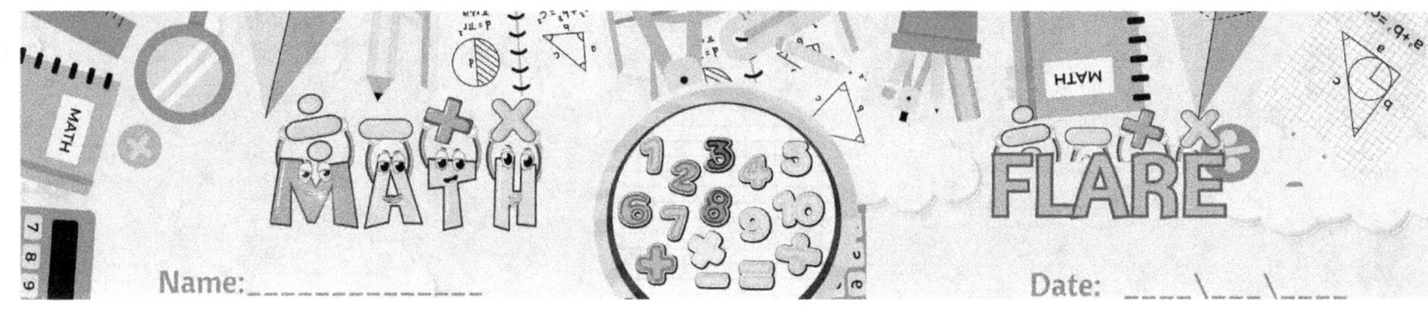

565. $(5^2) \times (7^2) + 11 =$

566. $(4^2) \times (18^2) + 13 =$

567. $10(7 + 19) =$

568. $6 \times (5 + 12) =$

569. $(6 + 9)^2 =$

570. $(18 + 4) \times (10 + 2) =$

571. $(2 + 16) \times (13 + 10) =$

572. $(20^2) \times (7^2) + 1 =$

573. $10 \times (4 + 12) =$

574. $(19^2) \times (7^2) + 17 =$

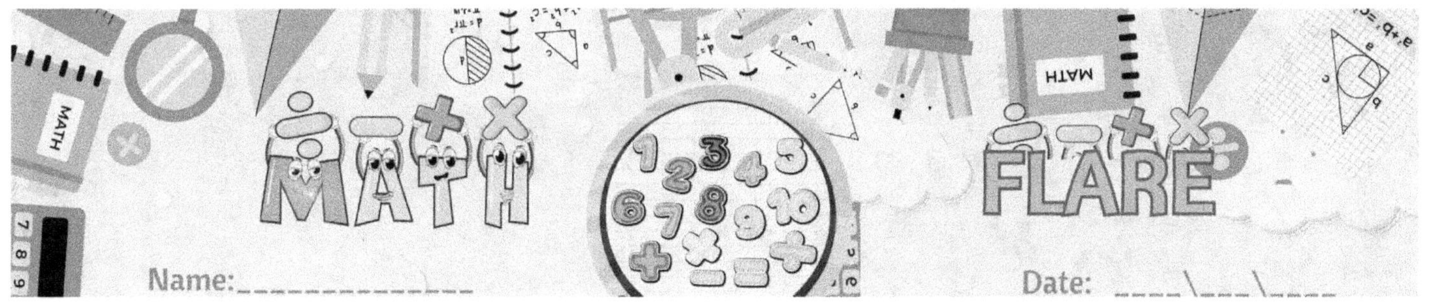

575. $14 \times (1 + 9) =$

576. $(13 \times 18) - (12 + 8) =$

577. $11 \times 18 =$

578. $5 + 17 + 15 =$

579. $3 \times 12 + 16 =$

580. $(9 + 3)(16 + 19) =$

581. $4 \times 5 + 5 =$

582. $(19^2) \times (14^2) + 16 =$

583. $8 + 5^2 =$

584. $4 \times 8 \times 9 =$

585. $(19^2) \times (8^2) + 13 =$

586. $10 \times 12 + 12 =$

587. $(18 + 17)^2 =$

588. $(20 + 13)(2 + 12) =$

589. $(4 + 12) \div 16 =$

590. $15 \times 17 + 16 =$

591. $6 + 2^2 =$

592. $2 + 17 - 1 + 4 =$

593. $12 + 9^2 =$

594. $2 \times 15 + 17 =$

ANSWERS

Page 1: Positive and Negative Integers

1. 9	2. -5	3. -15	4. -3	5. 24	6. -37	7. -1
8. 5	9. -33	10. -1	11. -25	12. -8	13. -16	14. 17
15. -7	16. -36	17. -11	18. 17	19. -6	20. 9	21. -6
22. -28	23. 0	24. -9	25. -33	26. 5	27. 16	28. 9
29. -13	30. -3	31. 0	32. 6	33. -9	34. -1	35. -8
36. -20	37. 24	38. 17	39. 11	40. 7	41. 22	42. 10
43. -27	44. -11	45. -44	46. 20	47. 10	48. 11	49. -15
50. -22	51. 13	52. -19	53. 19	54. -12	55. 0	56. 13
57. -35	58. -27	59. 17	60. 13	61. 16	62. 8	63. -4
64. 17	65. 31	66. -19	67. 5	68. -7	69. 8	70. 6
71. -28	72. -15	73. -37	74. 27	75. 10	76. 14	77. -14
78. -32	79. 21	80. -28	81. -15	82. -28	83. 0	84. 17
85. -2	86. -19	87. -26	88. 27	89. 18	90. -20	91. -37
92. -5	93. -26	94. -3	95. 10	96. -16	97. -13	98. 7
99. -34	100. -14	101. -21	102. -7	103. 12	104. 6	105. -4
106. 3	107. 11	108. 1	109. 0	110. 14	111. -3	112. 16
113. 8	114. -25	115. 8	116. 7	117. -7	118. 26	119. -24
120. -6	121. 32	122. 2	123. 5	124. 13	125. -17	126. 7
127. -4	128. -1	129. 23	130. 9	131. 9	132. -21	133. 23

134. 15   135. 27   136. 7   137. -40   138. -38   139. 5   140. -1

141. -19   142. -8   143. -19   144. 4   145. 4   146. -3   147. -7

148. 11   149. 7   150. -3   151. 17   152. 2   153. -6   154. -44

155. 20   156. -17   157. -11   158. 14   159. -6   160. -29   161. 4

162. 11   163. 13   164. 35   165. 4   166. 26   167. -21   168. -8

169. -18   170. -3   171. -1   172. 0   173. 31   174. -3   175. 4

176. 5   177. 30   178. 4   179. 13   180. -19   181. -23   182. 31

183. 11   184. -44   185. -4   186. 13   187. -8   188. 18   189. 26

190. 28   191. 4   192. -8   193. -38   194. 27   195. -11   196. 21

197. -24   198. 4   199. 19   200. -10

Page 21: Positive and Negative Integers

201. -32   202. -6   203. -4   204. 30   205. -21   206. 18   207. -33

208. 16   209. -6   210. -12   211. 27   212. -17   213. 12   214. -12

215. 41   216. -40   217. -10   218. -3   219. -21   220. -24   221. -25

222. 12   223. 14   224. 17   225. -29   226. -9   227. 12   228. 1

229. -42   230. 9   231. 2   232. -4   233. -6   234. -8   235. -17

236. 8   237. 0   238. 12   239. 5   240. 5   241. 12   242. -13

243. -30   244. -25   245. -12   246. -16   247. 21   248. 42   249. -9

250. -3   251. -19   252. -20   253. 12   254. 5   255. 8   256. 29

257. -20   258. -7   259. 17   260. 2   261. 17   262. 8   263. 22

264. 11   265. -11   266. -21   267. -10   268. -4   269. 10   270. -29

271. 10   272. -13   273. 2   274. -5   275. 3   276. -12   277. 8

278. -28   279. -2   280. 4   281. -19   282. 17   283. 22   284. 9

285. -5   286. 4   287. -32   288. -4   289. 12   290. -18   291. 26

292. -11   293. -6   294. -22   295. 20   296. 21   297. -28   298. -22

299. 18   300. 37   301. -12   302. 25   303. 14   304. 12   305. 32

306. -8   307. 19   308. -5   309. 2   310. 27   311. 1   312. -24

313. -21   314. -34   315. 4   316. -9   317. 0   318. 34   319. 33

320. 14   321. 10   322. -12   323. 39   324. 17   325. -10   326. -23

327. 9   328. -44   329. 30   330. 14   331. -22   332. 19   333. -4

334. -31   335. -7   336. 17   337. 12   338. 2   339. -6   340. -23

341. -15   342. -10   343. -21   344. -13   345. -10   346. 12   347. -11

348. 15   349. -8   350. 40   351. 22   352. -17   353. 14   354. -6

355. 2   356. -11   357. 18   358. -6   359. 19   360. -11   361. 27

362. -8   363. 26   364. -1   365. 10   366. 6   367. 23   368. 6

369. -3   370. -28   371. 18   372. 24   373. -17   374. 8   375. 0

376. 5   377. 18   378. 27   379. -26   380. 3   381. 7   382. 8

383. 2   384. 23   385. 21   386. -19   387. -7   388. -25   389. 43

390. -4   391. -2   392. 17   393. 1   394. 2   395. -5   396. -26

Page 41: Order of Operations (PEMDAS)

397. 4   398. 562   399. 124   400. 81

401. 15,879   402. 33,138   403. 93   404. 132

405. 196
406. 150
407. 442
408. 28
409. 3.1
410. 23
411. 336
412. 308
413. 2.2
414. 33
415. 15,878
416. 126
417. 270
418. 7,752
419. 50
420. 1
421. 54,771
422. 65,030
423. 12,551
424. 17
425. 261
426. 196
427. 92,427
428. 38
429. 11
430. 41
431. 1,640
432. 72
433. 40
434. 9
435. 10,422
436. 7,059
437. 42
438. 6.8
439. 48
440. 14
441. 333
442. 435
443. 154
444. 1,282
445. 30,986
446. 294
447. 36
448. 430
449. 200
450. 49
451. 1,547
452. 929
453. 236
454. -8
455. 1,261
456. 32
457. 198
458. 3.8
459. 47
460. 3.2
461. 0.3
462. 180
463. 35
464. 84
465. 1.4
466. 6,403
467. 32
468. 171
469. 7
470. 255
471. 26
472. 85
473. 1,088
474. 12
475. 137
476. 2,925
477. 841
478. 31
479. 961
480. 21
481. 480
482. 18
483. 441
484. 6,570
485. 130
486. 38
487. 99
488. 2,120

489. 29

490. 270

491. 868

492. 17,429

493. 840

494. 40

495. 1,378

496. 459

497. 135

498. 450

499. 220

500. 51

501. 24

502. 484

503. 234

504. 89

505. 70

506. 266

507. 234

508. 37

509. 2,321

510. 104,984

511. 19

512. 326

513. 587

514. 39

515. 55

516. 29

517. 144,403

518. 18

519. 187

520. 243

521. 57,614

522. 1.5

523. 90

524. 144

525. 47

526. 432

527. 6

528. 43

529. 320

530. 22

531. 432

532. 9

533. 30,989

534. 368

535. 28

536. 800

537. 8,116

538. 44

539. 48,850

540. 67

541. 57

542. 0.7

543. 6,413

544. 544

545. 726

546. 47

547. 15

548. 336

549. 204

550. 133

551. 36

552. 85

553. 17

554. 399

555. 9

556. 20

557. 24

558. 180

559. 80

560. 119

561. 38

562. 24,339

563. 104

564. 63

565. 1,236

566. 5,197

567. 260

568. 102

569. 225

570. 264

571. 414

572. 19,601

573. 160

574. 17,706

575. 140

576. 214

577. 198

578. 37

579. 52

580. 420

581. 25

582. 70,772

583. 33

584. 288

585. 23,117

586. 132

587. 1,225

588. 462

589. 1

590. 271

591. 10

592. 22

593. 93

594. 47